Excavations at Wyndyke Furlong, Abingdon, Oxfordshire, 1994

by Jeff Muir and Mark R Roberts

With contributions by Kate Atherton, Alistair Barclay, Angela Boyle, Philippa Bradley, Jenny Robinson, Fiona Roe, Chris Salter, Jane R Timby and Bob Wilson (with Alison Locker)

Thames Valley Landscapes Monograph No. 12
1999

Published by the Oxford Archaeological Unit
with the Oxford University Committee for
Archaeology

ISBN 0-947816-90-9

Printed in Great Britain
by
UNiSKill Ltd, Eynsham, Oxon

The OAU would like to acknowledge the support of Standard Life Assurance Company during this project, and their financial assistance with the cost of publication.

CONTENTS

CHAPTER 1: INTRODUCTION *by Jeff Muir*
Summary
Location and geology
Archaeological and historical background
Project background 1
The evaluation
Excavation methodology 2
Report structure 3

CHAPTER 2: ARCHAEOLOGICAL DESCRIPTION *by Jeff Muir*
Trench 29
The middle to late Iron Age
Waterhole 29/9 and ditches 29/88 and 29/50
Posthole cluster
Undated features
Ditches 29/90 and 29/68 5
Ditches 29/15 and 29/21
Trench 32 6
The middle Iron Age
Enclosure 3556 (gullies 3403, 3561 and 3560) 7
The Roman period
1st – 2nd century AD
Ditch 3563
Ditch 3432
Earlier 2nd century AD
Ditch 3205
Ditch 3564
Ditch 3566
Ditch 3567
Metalled surface 3532
Later 2nd century AD
Feature 3562 (ditches 3235 and 3550)
Gully complex 3568 9
The medieval period
Ditch 3230
Ditch 3226
Ditch 3414
Ditches 3306 and 3446
Undated features
Trench 33
The earlier prehistoric period
Ditch 5961
Ditch 6305 11
The early to middle Iron Age
Possible post-built circular structures
Structures 5257 and 5087
Structure 5166
Structure 6310 15
Other post-built structures
Structure 6313
Ditched circular structures
Structure 6286 16
Structure 6287
Other features
Ditches 6308 and 6309
The middle Iron Age
The roundhouses
Structure 5021 17
Structure 6282 19
Structure 6283 20
Structure 6286
Structure 6290
Structure 6291
Structure 6295
Structure 6297
Windbreak features 22
Structures 6072, 6306 and 6307
Structure 6301
Boundary ditch 6298
Ditch 6299
Ditch complex 6300 23
Well 5664
The Roman period
Enclosure 5978
Ditch 5359 24
Pits
Method and classification
Environmental evidence
Chronology
Postholes 25
Posthole alignment 6312
Posthole cluster 6313
Posthole clusters 6314 and 6315
Posthole cluster 6316
Posthole cluster 6317 26

CHAPTER 3: THE FINDS
The pottery *by Jane R Timby*
Introduction
Methodology
Discussion
Earlier prehistoric pottery 31
Iron Age pottery
Early Iron Age pottery 32
Middle Iron Age pottery 35

Later Iron Age – Roman pottery 37
Summary
Catalogue of illustrated sherds
Bronze Age 38
Early-middle Iron Age 39
Roman
The worked flint *by Philippa Bradley*
Introduction 40
Technology and dating
Discussion 41
Catalogue of illustrated pieces
The fired clay *by Alistair Barclay*
Introduction
Method
Fabrics
Loomweights 42
Plates and miscellaneous objects
Structural clay
Hearth/oven clay
Miscellaneous
Discussion 43
The worked stone *by Fiona Roe*
Introduction
The Iron Age
The Roman period
Discussion
The Iron Age 44
The Roman period
The small finds *by Kate Atherton*
Introduction
Copper alloy 46
Iron 47
Bone 48
Other material
Discussion 49
The metal-working debris *by Chris Salter*
The wider context 50

CHAPTER 4: THE HUMAN, PLANT AND ANIMAL REMAINS
The human remains *by Angela Boyle*
Discussion
Macroscopic plant and invertebrate remains *by Jenny Robinson*
Introduction
Methods and results 51
Interpretation
The Iron Age 53
The Roman period 56
The animal bone *by Bob Wilson with Alison Locker*
Introduction
Numbers of bone fragments 58
Skeletons, articulated bone groups and crania
Information on age at death of animals 59
Bone measurements
Pathology 60

CHAPTER 5: DISCUSSION AND CONCLUSIONS *by Jeff Muir*
Introduction
Earlier prehistoric activity
The Iron Age
The early settlement
Post-built structures 61
The developed settlement
The roundhouses
Possible windbreak features 62
Pits
Postholes
Boundaries and waterholes
Settlement layout
Site economy and status
Agriculture 63
Animal husbandry
Special animal deposits
Domestic industry
Trade and exchange 64
Abandonment
The Romano-British period
Economic change and development 65

APPENDICES
Appendix A: Fabric descriptions
Later prehistoric 67
Roman 68
Appendix B: Concordance of contexts, features and structures containing artefacts and environmental samples 70

BIBLIOGRAPHY 73

LIST OF FIGURES

Figure 1.1 Site location and archaeological background viii

Figure 1.2 Local geology 2

Figure 1.3 Trench location plan 3

Figure 2.1 Trench 29, all periods 4

Figure 2.2 Section through waterhole 29/9 5

Figure 2.3 Trench 32, all periods 6

Figure 2.4 Middle Iron Age enclosure 3556 7

Figure 2.5 The Roman period, 1st – 2nd century AD 8

Figure 2.6 The medieval field system 10

Figure 2.7 Trench 33, all periods 12

Figure 2.8 Earlier prehistoric activity (Trench 33) 13

Figure 2.9 Early to middle Iron Age activity (Trench 33) 14

Figure 2.10 Early to middle Iron Age post-built structures 15

Figure 2.11 Structure 6286 16

Figure 2.12 Gully profiles, structure 6286 17

Figure 2.13 Middle Iron Age activity (Trench 33) 18

Figure 2.14 Structure 5021 19

Figure 2.15 Structures 6282 and 6283 20

Figure 2.16 Structures 6290, 6291 and 6295 and middle Iron Age pits 21

Figure 2.17 Section through gullies 5839 and 5316 22

Figure 2.18 Structure 6297 and windbreak feature 6072 23

Figure 2.19 Boundary ditch 6298 and well 5664 24

Figure 2.20 Section through boundary ditch 6299 25

Figure 2.21 Section through well 5664 26

Figure 2.22 The Roman period (Trench 33) 27

Figure 2.23 Pit distribution, all periods (Trench 33) 28

Figure 2.24 Posthole distribution, all periods (Trench 33) 29

Figure 3.1 Bronze Age pottery (1–4) 30

Figure 3.2 Iron Age pottery (5–21) 33

Figure 3.3 Iron Age pottery (22–34) 34

Figure 3.4 Iron Age pottery (35–44) 36

Figure 3.5 Roman pottery (45–50) 38

Figure 3.6 Worked Flint (1–4) 41

Figure 3.7 Small finds (1–4) 47

LIST OF TABLES

Table 2.1 Excavated pits (by phase) 25

Table 2.2 Postholes containing pottery (by phase) 25

Table 3.1 Structures and features with 20 or more sherds from early and middle Iron Age periods 30

Table 3.2 Total quantities of later Prehistoric pottery 32

Table 3.3 Quantities of Iron Age fabrics from phased contexts (excluding re-deposited or unphased material) 35

Table 3.4 Total quantities of later Iron Age / Roman wares 37

Table 3.5 Worked flint assemblage composition 40

Table 3.6 Summary and quantification of all fired clay by type 42

Table 3.7 Comparison of all identified loomweights 43

Table 3.8 Ashville: Iron Age stone 44

Table 3.9 Wyndyke Furlong: Iron Age stone 45

Table 3.10 Ashville: Roman stone 45

Table 3.11 Wyndyke Furlong: Roman stone 46

Table 3.12 Weight of metal-working debris types by period 50

Table 4.1 Waterlogged macroscopic plant remains from the late Iron Age well 29/9 52

Table 4.2 Charred plant material from the late Iron Age well 29/9 53

Table 4.3 Molluscs 54

Table 4.4a Early and middle Iron Age charred plant remains 55

Table 4.4b Early and middle Iron Age charred plant remains 56

Table 4.4c Early and middle Iron Age charred plant remains 57

Table 4.5 Late Iron Age and Roman charred plant remains 57

Table 4.6 Fragment frequency and percentage of animal bones according to period 58

Table 4.7 Fragment frequency and percentage of handpicked bones according to type of middle Iron Age feature in Trench 33 and according to soil sieving 59

Table 4.8 Grouped skeletal elements of sheep/goat bones from pits and ditches 59

Table 4.9 Mandible wear stages at death 59

Table 4.10 Bone measurements: greatest length of elements (GL) in mm 60

ACKNOWLEDGEMENTS

We are very grateful to Standard Life Assurance Company for funding the archaeological fieldwork and publication. Thanks to Hugh Coddington for ideas and helpful suggestions in the field. Thanks also to Angela Boyle of the Oxford Archaeological Unit (OAU) who monitored the crucial stages of post-excavation work. The illustrations are by Sam Potter, except for the small finds and flint which were drawn by Luke Adams. Corrections to the illustrations were made by M. Costello. The report was edited by Chris Hayden. Fiona Roe would like to thank Christine Edbury of the Oxford County Museum, Standlake, and Alison Roberts of the Ashmolean Museum, for enabling her to see worked stone from other Oxfordshire Iron Age and Roman sites.

LOCATION OF THE ARCHIVE

All original site records, including the finds and material generated during post-excavation analysis, have been deposited with the Oxfordshire Museums Service. A copy of the paper archive is also held on microfilm by the National Monuments Record, RCHM(E), Swindon.

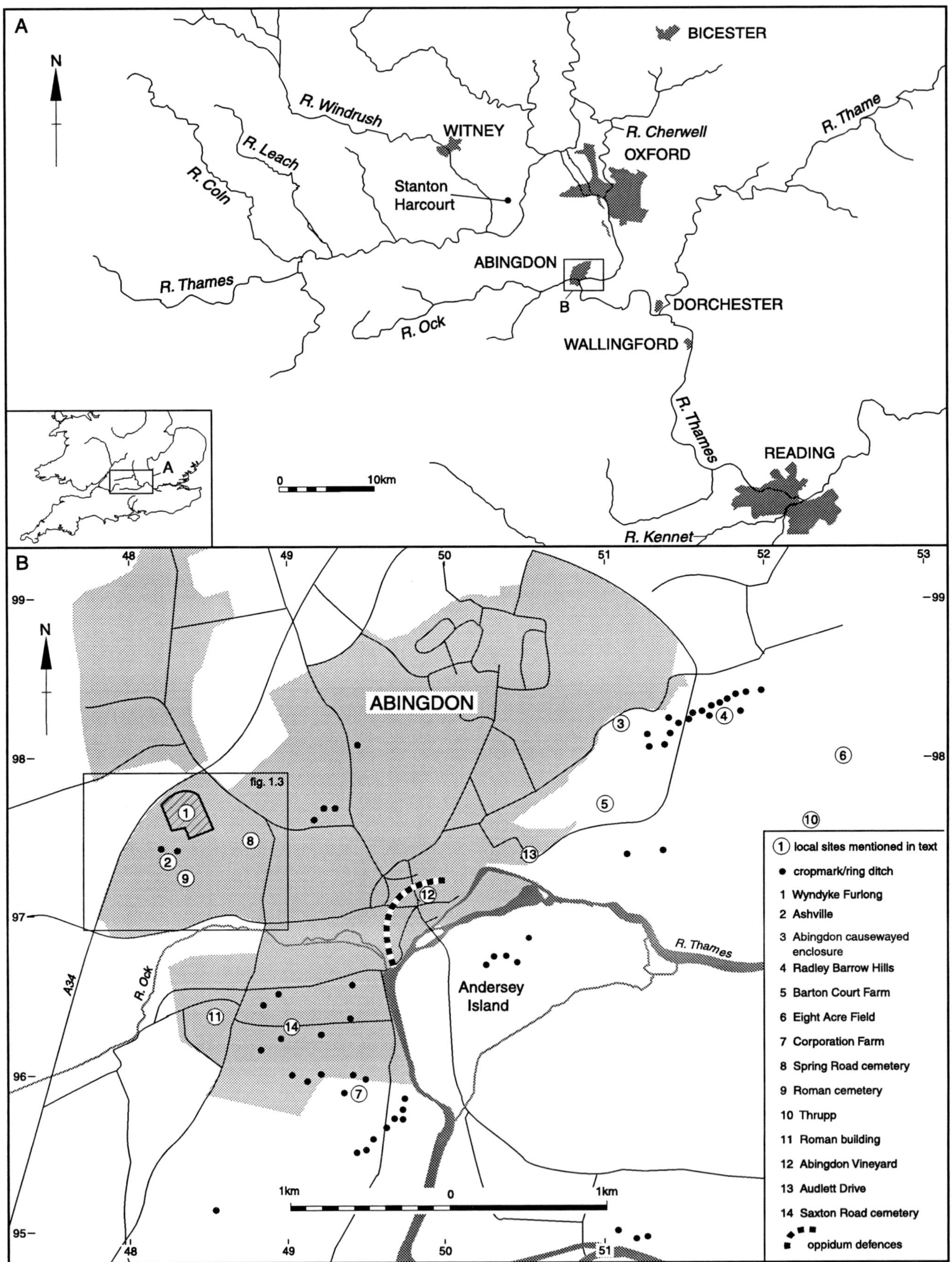

Figure 1.1 Site location and archaeological background

Chapter 1: Introduction

by Jeff Muir

SUMMARY

Excavations at Wyndyke Furlong were undertaken in advance of business park development on the site of the old Ashville Trading Estate, Abingdon. The work was funded by the Standard Life Assurance Company and revealed the substantial remains of a middle Iron Age settlement and early Roman field-system and droveway. The Iron Age settlement is the northern continuation of the middle Iron Age settlement excavated at Ashville by Parrington in the 1970s (Parrington 1978) and is the latest in a long series of investigations into the Iron Age landscape to the west of Abingdon.

LOCATION AND GEOLOGY

The Iron Age settlement at Wyndyke Furlong (NGR SU 4825 9772) was located on the Second Gravel Terrace, 1.2 km west of the centre of modern Abingdon, overlooking the confluence of the Rivers Thames and Ock (Fig. 1.1). The site may have been attractive to settlers because of its location, at the crest of a natural rise on the gravel terrace. At this point the gravel is very free draining. Immediately to the north of the site the terrace gives way to underlying lenses of gravel, impermeable clay and silt (Fig. 1.2). To the east, the settlement was bounded by the Larkhill Stream.

ARCHAEOLOGICAL AND HISTORICAL BACKGROUND

The site of Wyndyke Furlong lies in a landscape relatively rich in archaeological remains of all periods (Fig. 1.1). The area is perhaps best known for its prehistoric monuments such as the Abingdon causewayed enclosure (Avery 1982, 10-50) and the barrow cemetery at Barrow Hills, Radley (Barclay and Halpin 1999). The ring ditches at Barrow hills were not unique but formed a small part of a much wider cemetery first located as cropmarks on aerial photographs (Benson and Miles 1974, map 30). Two of these ring ditches were excavated at Ashville just to the south of Wyndyke Furlong in 1976 (Balkwill 1978, 25–30).

Evidence for Iron Age settlement has steadily accumulated over a number of years with the completion of evaluations and open-area excavations at Ashville (Parrington 1978), The MG Works (Halpin 1983; 1984; Roberts 1993), Barton Court Farm (Miles 1986) and Thrupp (Ainslie 1992, 63-5; Everett and Eeles 1999) (Figs 1.1 and 1.3). The varied nature of the settlement evidence argues for a well-developed, and in the case of Thrupp, a semi-specialised agricultural economy for the Iron Age. The gradual emergence of Abingdon within that economy as a high status defended site or oppidum has given the investigation of its hinterlands an important new focus of interest (Allen 1990b, 73–76; 1991, 97–99; 1993, 64–66; 1994, 33; 1996, 51–55; 1997a, 47–53).

Evidence for Roman occupation is also abundant in the region. In Abingdon itself Roman activity has been traced from the Abbey gardens in the east to beyond West St Helen Street in the west (Allen 1997a, 48). In 1968 part of a rectangular stone building was excavated at Masefield Cresent (SU485963) by the Abingdon Archaeological Society (NMR, UID 233998). The structure was associated with Roman building materials and 3rd – 4th century AD pottery. To the north-east of the town, the late Iron Age site at Barton Court Farm eventually emerged as a Roman villa (Miles 1986). Funerary evidence is also abundant. Two Roman cemeteries have been excavated at Barrow Hills (Atkinson 1952; Boyle and Chambers in prep.) and a third was revealed 200 m to the south of the Ashville site (Parrington 1978, 23–5).

Saxon activity in the Abingdon area is illustrated by the presence of both settlement and cemeteries. Evidence for early Saxon settlement, including several sunken featured buildings, was revealed at Audlett Drive on the eastern edge of the modern town (Keevil 1992, 55–79) and at the Vineyard (Allen 1990b, 74–5). Early Saxon occupation material was also recovered from the Spring Road municipal cemetery 400 m to the east of Wyndyke Furlong (Allen 1990c). More extensive settlement remains have also been excavated at Radley Barrow Hills (Boyle and Chambers in prep.) and at Barton Court Farm (Miles 1986). Further to the south-west, the large Saxon cemetery at Saxton Road contained over 100 inhumations and almost as many cremations (Dickinson 1976, 2.3–31). With the exception of documentary evidence concerning the refounding of Abingdon Abbey (see Biddle *et al.* 1968, appndx 2 for sources), evidence for later Saxon activity in the town and in the Abingdon area is limited.

PROJECT BACKGROUND

The excavations at Wyndyke Furlong were undertaken on behalf of Standard Life Assurance Company in advance of business park development. The development area was known to be of archaeological importance following a series of excavations and evaluations conducted largely by the Oxford Archaeological Unit (OAU) in response to piecemeal development of the Ashville Trading Estate (Fig. 1.3; Parrington 1978; Halpin 1983; 1984; 1985; Roberts 1993; 1994).

The first major excavations at Ashville were conducted under salvage conditions between 1974 and 1976 by the Abingdon and District Archaeological Society under the direction of Michael Parrington of the OAU (Parrington 1978). The excavations revealed a

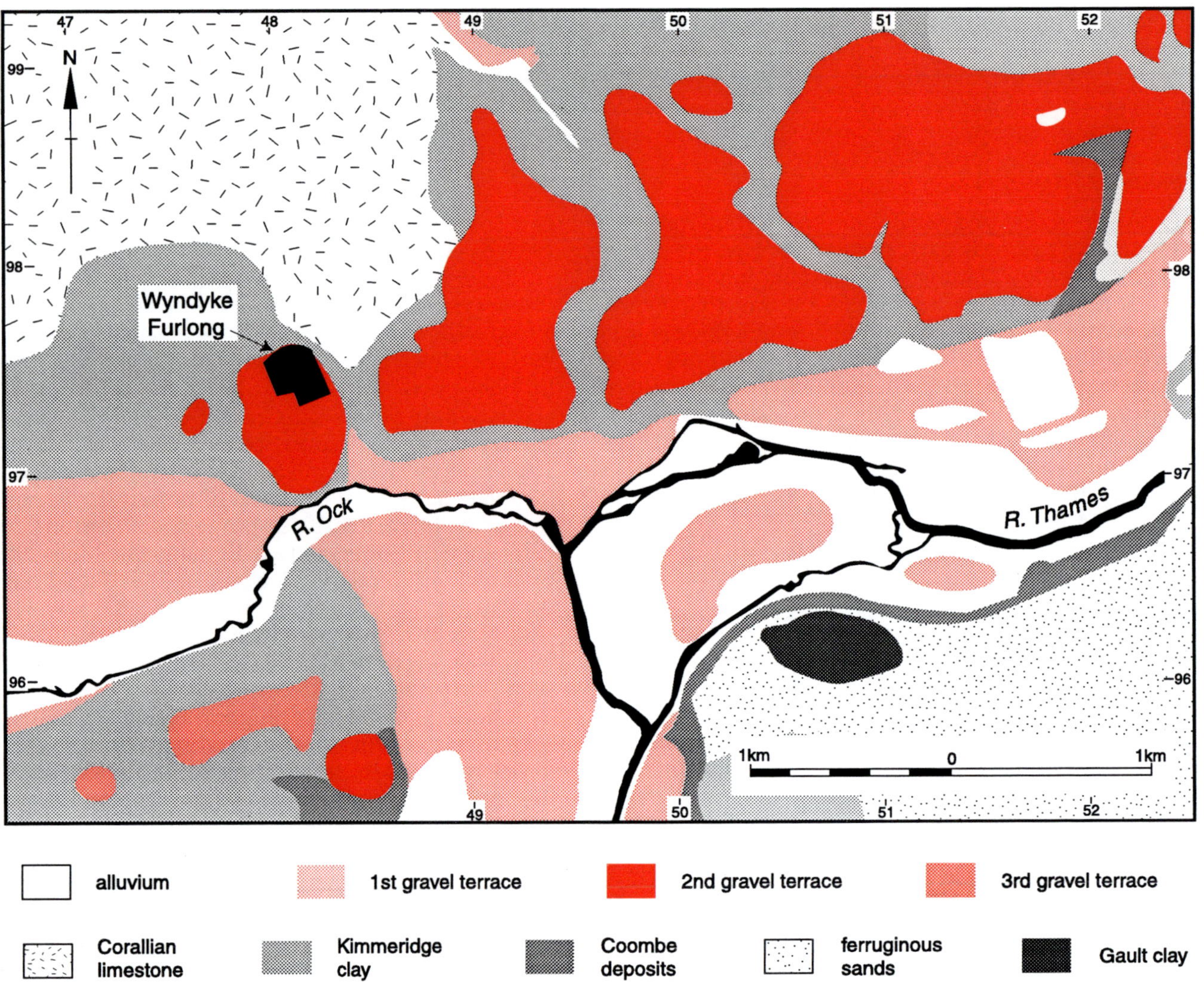

Figure 1.2 Local geology

considerable density of features ranging from funerary monuments of the late Bronze Age to field systems of the early Roman period. The majority of features, however, were dated to the Iron Age. They consisted of house gullies, pits and postholes which formed a settlement covering an area of over 5000 m^2.

In subsequent years, the southern extent of what was believed to be the same settlement was defined *c* 150 m to the south-west by a pair of evaluations conducted by Claire Halpin (OAU) at Blacklands Furlong (Halpin 1983; 1984) and on the site of the MG car factory (Halpin 1985). An evaluation conducted by Mark Roberts (OAU) to the east of the MG works revealed very little of archaeological interest (Roberts 1993).

THE EVALUATION

In October 1994 a further evaluation was undertaken by Mark Roberts ahead of the proposed new development of the Business Park at Wyndyke Furlong (Roberts 1994). The evaluation consisted of 15 trenches, each 30 m in length and 1.3 m wide, providing a 1% sample of the development area. The trenches revealed a dense continuation of the Ashville settlement to the north, a separate area of field ditches, and a focus of Romano-British activity 300 m to the north-east of that. As a result of the evaluation, these three areas were targeted for further excavation, the results of which form the basis of this report.

EXCAVATION METHODOLOGY

Following the initial evaluation, the area of field ditches was investigated by a further sixteen evaluation trenches. Trench 29 contained an Iron Age waterhole and was eventually expanded to cover an area of *c* 335 m^2. In addition to the evaluation trenches, two larger, open-area trenches were located in order to examine the Romano-British activity (Trench 32, *c* 3330 m^2) and the area of dense Iron Age occupation (Trench 33, *c* 2760 m^2). Both trenches were stripped of topsoil using a 360° mechanical excavator under archaeological supervision. All archaeological features were then planned at a scale of 1:50.

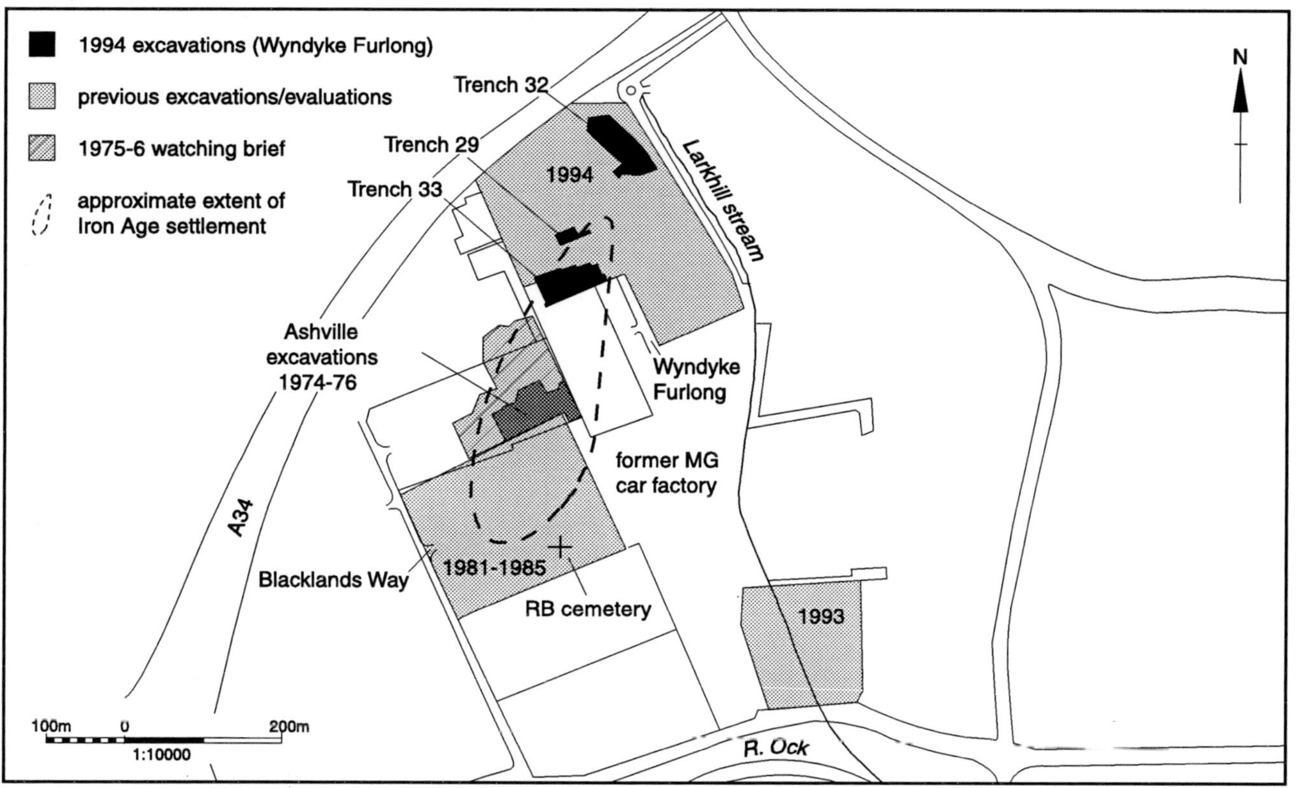

Figure 1.3 Trench location plan

The density of features in Trench 33 was so great that although all were planned, only a targeted selection of features was excavated. Subcircular features such as pits and postholes were generally half-sectioned and linear features sampled appropriately with the principal aims of unravelling stratigraphic relationships and recovering dateable artefacts. All features were excavated by hand. A series of circular gullies in Trench 33 were targeted for the most intensive excavation. It was thought that the gullies marked house sites and were, therefore, likely to prove rich in artefacts. Pits, postholes and other features were selected for excavation with the specific aim of creating as balanced a coverage as possible across the site.

Environmental sampling was carried out wherever features showed particular promise with minimal sampling of other features. It was hoped that the Iron Age waterhole located in Trench 29 would provide a useful sequence of waterlogged remains to compare with the data recovered from the Ashville excavations (Chapter 4).

REPORT STRUCTURE

In the archaeological description of the site (Chapter 2), the site is described chronologically, trench by trench. The archaeology of Trench 29 is thus discussed first, then Trench 32 and finally Trench 33. Because Trench 29 was in effect an expanded evaluation trench all context numbers are prefixed with the Trench number (29) in order to distinguish the contexts from other trenches held in the archive. Trench 32 was assigned a unique block of context numbers (3200–3999) in order to easily distinguish it from Trench 33 contexts, which were similarly assigned a separate block of numbers (5000–6999). Unless otherwise indicated, numbers in the text prefixed by F refer to individual features (eg a pit or ditch); those prefixed by S to larger 'structures' consisting of a number of associated features (eg a roundhouse consisting of gullies, postholes and pits). Numbers without such prefixes refer to individual contexts (eg a single layer within a pit). Chapter 2 is not intended to provide a full level three description of the archaeology, but should be viewed as a synthetic overview of the more salient features which help to characterise the settlement. The specialists reports have been grouped together to form Chapters 3 (the finds) and 4 (the human, plant and animal remains) which have been published in condensed form. Although the nature of this report precludes a full synthesis of the Ashville/Wyndyke excavations, a brief comparative analysis has been undertaken and integrated into the discussion and conclusions which form Chapter 5.

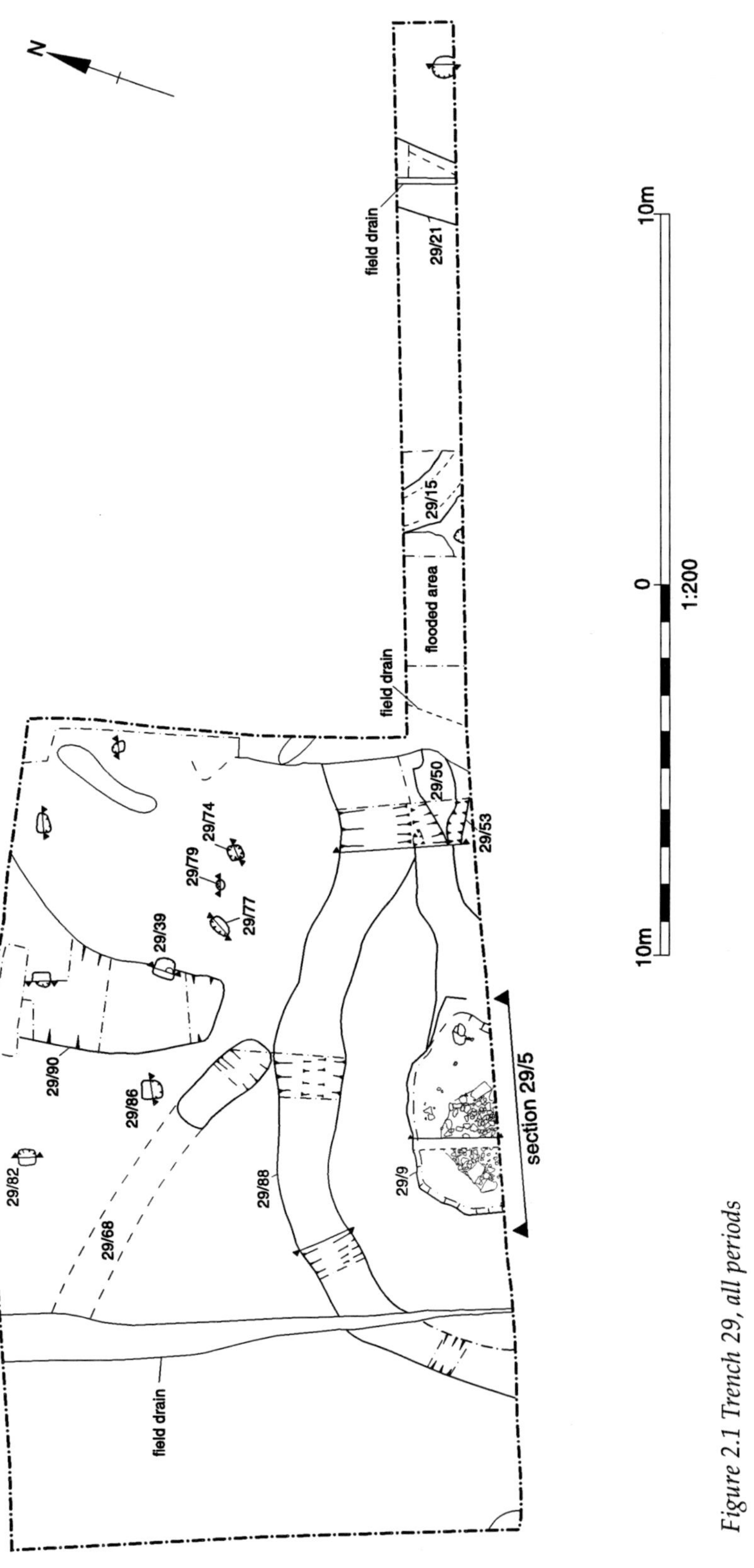

Figure 2.1 Trench 29, all periods

Chapter 2: Archaeological Description

by Jeff Muir

TRENCH 29

Trench 29 contained a large well or waterhole (29/9), surrounded by a ditch (29/88; Fig. 2.1). To the north of the waterhole were a number of postholes which may have formed a timber structure or fenceline.

The middle to late Iron Age

Waterhole 29/9 and ditches 29/88 and 29/50 (*Fig. 2.1*)

Waterhole (29/9) was located towards the south-western end of Trench 29. The feature was partially obscured by the edge of the excavation but was approximately oval in plan, with a visible extent of *c* 7 x 3 m. Only the top 1.3 m of this feature was excavated due to flooding. The earliest fills (29/23–29/25) consisted of dark grey sandy silts with occasional blocks of limestone (Fig. 2.2). This sequence was sealed by a thick layer of clay silt (29/11) which contained a considerable quantity of limestone rubble, apparently thrown in as an attempt to backfill the feature. This in turn was covered by a mixed layer of clay loam with gravel (29/6). Two of the earliest deposits which were excavated (29/23 and 29/24) contained late Iron Age pottery, and it is probable that the well was backfilled during this period. It may have been open and was presumably also in use during the middle Iron Age.

A curvilinear ditch (29/88) lay immediately to the north of the waterhole. The ditch curved around the waterhole at its south-western end, clearly respecting the larger feature. The ditch had a U-shaped profile with a rounded bottom and gradually sloping sides. It was 1.3 m wide and filled with deposits of silty clay. Four segments were excavated through the ditch, all of which contained late Iron Age pottery. The purpose of the ditch is unclear, but it may have been dug in order to keep livestock away from the waterhole after it had been backfilled when the ground may have been dangerously boggy. At its eastern end, the ditch was cut by a narrower ditch (29/50) which was also dated to the late Iron Age. This feature was linear in plan and oriented north-east - south-west. Its south-western end was lost in the fill of waterhole 29/9.

Posthole cluster (*Fig. 2.1*)

Approximately 2 m to the north of the waterhole and ditch was a group of nine postholes of various shapes and dimensions. Five of the postholes (29/74, 29/79, 29/77, 29/39 and 29/86) ran roughly parallel with ditch 29/88 and could be interpreted as a fenceline or boundary. It is also possible, however, that some or all of the postholes formed part of a structure or building of uncertain plan. Two of the postholes (29/82 and 29/74) contained pottery dating to the early/middle and middle Iron Age respectively.

Undated features

Ditches 29/90 and 29/68 (*Fig. 2.1*)

Ditches 29/68 and 29/90 were shallow features (0.12 – 0.20 m deep) of uncertain date and function. Ditch 29/68 was 1 m wide and was oriented north-west – south-east. It was badly truncated and only survived to the north-east as a stain in the gravel. Ditch 29/90 was *c* 2.6 m wide and curved away from a square terminal towards the north-east. Both features terminated near to the northern edge of ditch 29/88 and appeared to respect it. Neither feature contained pottery.

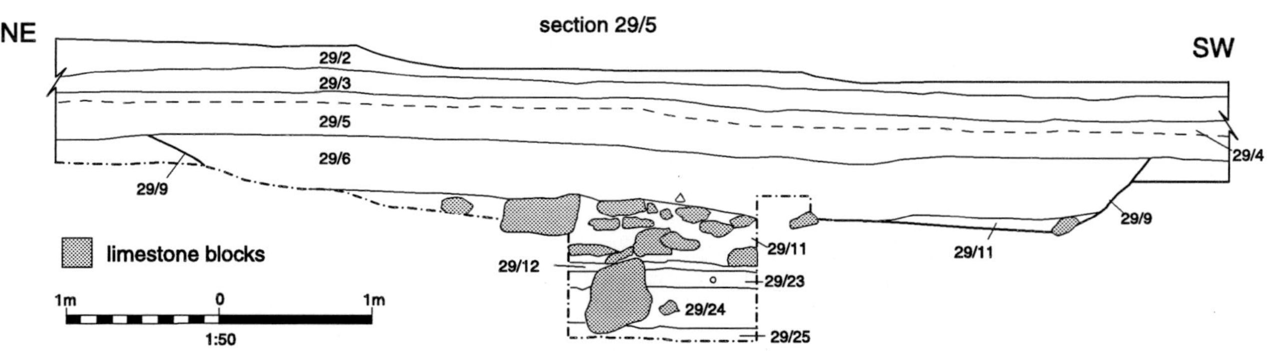

Figure 2.2 Section through waterhole 29/9

Ditches 29/15 and 29/21 *(Fig. 2.1)*

Two ditched features located towards the north-eastern end of the trench (29/15 and 29/21) were not excavated due to the high water table. Ditch 29/15 (1 m wide) appeared to be curvilinear in plan and measured 1 m wide. It is possible that the feature was originally circular or penannular, though there was no visible return of the ditch to the north-east. Ditch 29/21 appeared to be linear in plan, measured 1.6 m wide and was oriented approximately north-south. The centre of the feature was disturbed by a modern field drain.

TRENCH 32 *(Fig. 2.3)*

The archaeology within Trench 32 consisted of a middle Iron Age enclosure which was overlain by a Roman field system and associated trackway dating to the 1st–2nd century AD. The Roman field system was itself superseded by a new pattern of fields dating to the medieval period.

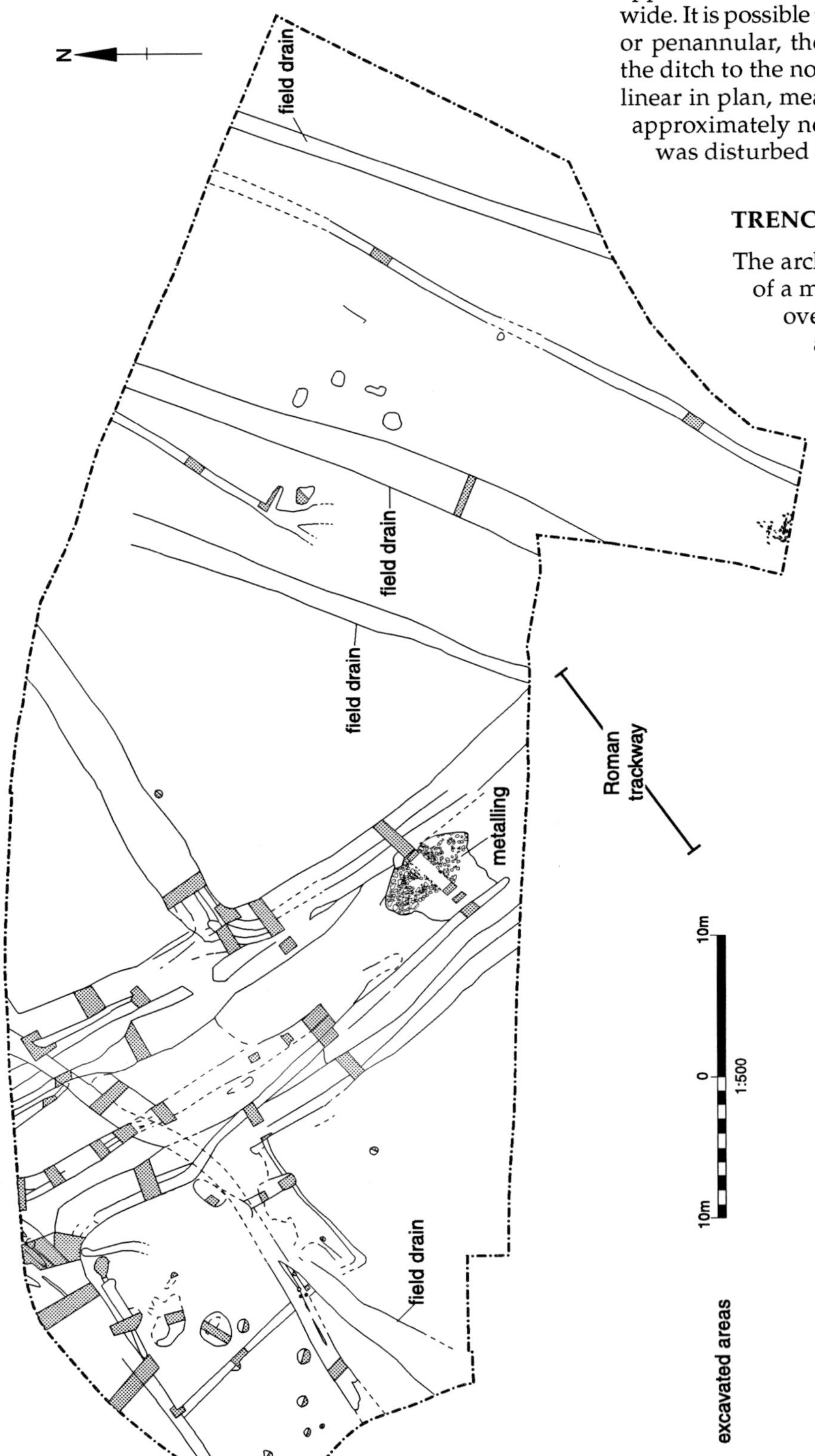

Figure 2.3 Trench 32, all periods

The middle Iron Age

Enclosure 3556 (Gullies 3403, 3561 and 3560) (Fig. 2.4)

Feature 3556 was a subrectangular enclosure which has been tentatively ascribed to the middle Iron Age on the strength of a small number of pottery sherds and its position within a limited stratigraphic sequence. The enclosure consisted of a narrow, V-shaped gully 3403 (0.60 m wide x 0.25 m deep) which formed its western and southern sides, a similar gully (3561) which may have demarcated the northern side and three intercutting gullies to the east (3557, 3558 and 3559=3560). The enclosure was 17 x 14 m wide internally. Ditch 3403 which formed most of the enclosure, contained a small amount of middle Iron Age pottery. The ditch was truncated at its south-eastern and northern limits by a sequence of ditches dated to the 2nd century AD. Ditch 3403 did not appear to connect directly with the eastern arm of the enclosure (3560) and it is possible that there was an entrance at this point.

Ditch 3561 on the northern side of the enclosure has been included as part of the feature largely because its form and depth were similar to 3403. No pottery was recovered from the ditch, however, and its orientation was slightly skew to the rest of the enclosure. If the ditch was part of the enclosure, it terminated short of the eastern ditch 3560 leaving a gap of 6 m.

Ditch 3560 was visible from the northern baulk of the trench towards the south-east for a distance of 32 m. It consisted of an original gully which had been heavily truncated by two recuts. The ditch was of variable width and depth, measuring some 0.50–0.70 m wide x 0.10–0.30 m deep. The inclusion of 3560 as part of the rectangular enclosure 3556 is speculative and based on the recovery of a small amount of middle Iron Age pottery. If the pottery was redeposited then 3560 could have been part of the later Roman trackway, perhaps twinned with the 1st century AD ditch 3563 (Fig. 2.5). If so, this would mean that the enclosure 3556 was a three-sided structure or that a fourth side had been obliterated by the later Roman trackway ditches.

A group of small pits or postholes was located to the west of enclosure 3556. The postholes were of varying sizes and shapes and did not form any coherent structure (see Chapter 5). A number of subcircular features located within the enclosure proved to be tree-throw holes.

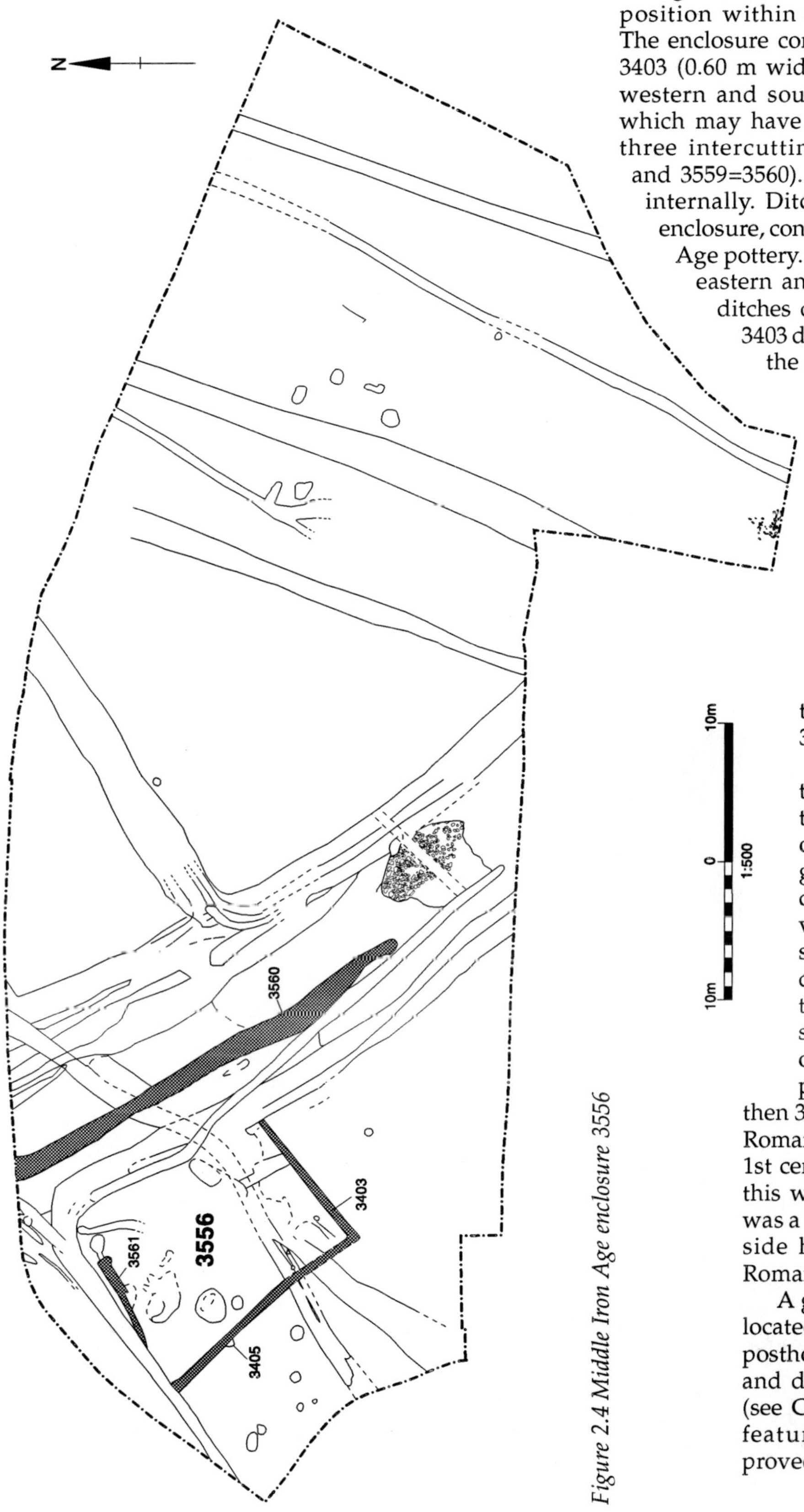

Figure 2.4 Middle Iron Age enclosure 3556

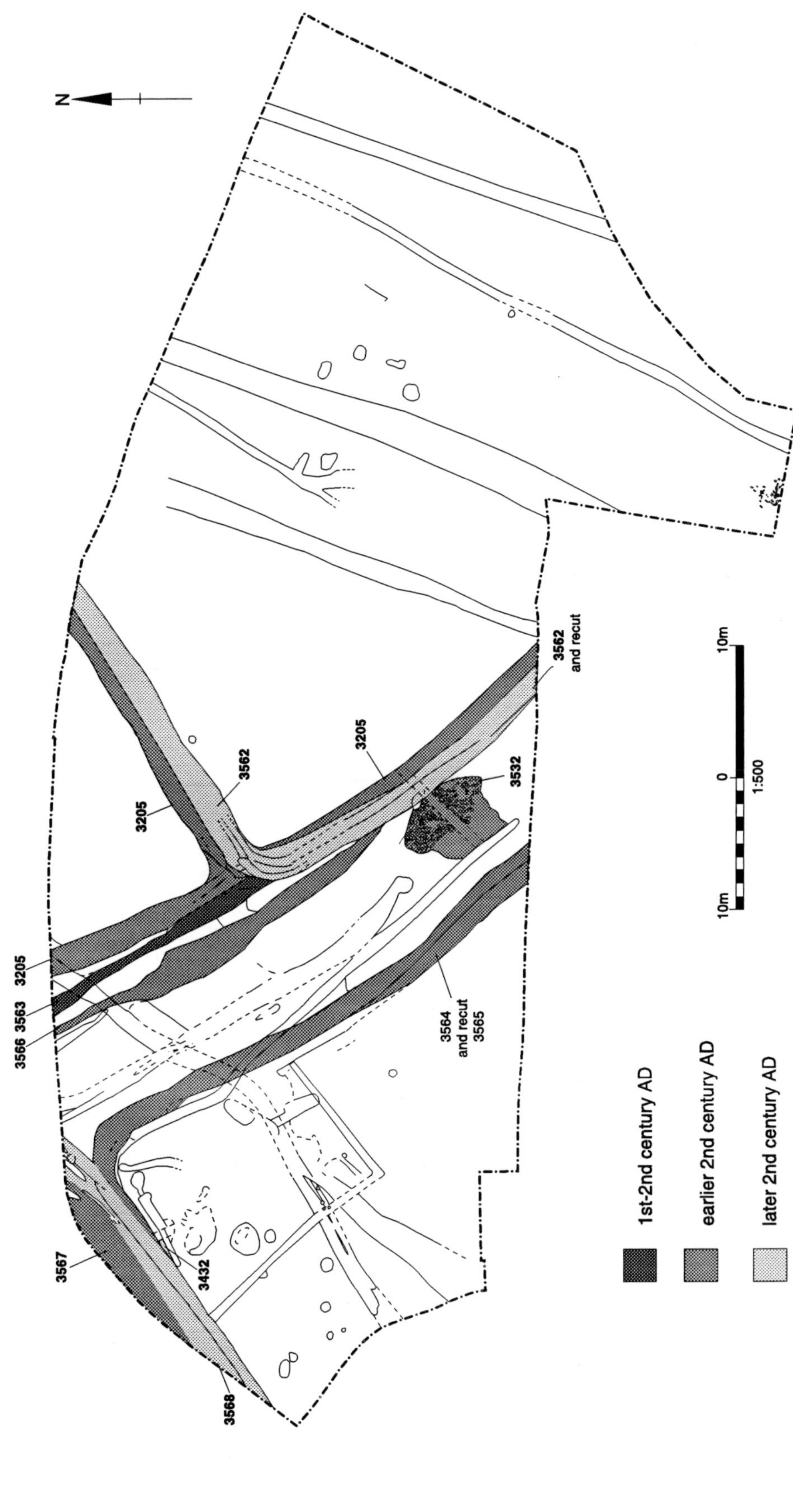

Figure 2.5 The Roman period, 1st – 2nd century AD

The Roman period

Trench 32 was dominated by a ditched trackway and associated field system dated to the 1st and 2nd centuries AD. Due to the intercutting nature of the archaeology and the very similar composition of ditch fills, the precise stratigraphic sequence proved difficult to establish. The broader picture of an evolving Roman agricultural landscape is clear enough, however. Given the presence and orientation of the middle Iron Age enclosure 3556 it is probable that the Roman trackway began as a less developed boundary or trackway during the Iron Age.

1st – 2nd century AD *(Fig. 2.5)*

Ditch 3563

Ditch 3563 marked the eastern side of the trackway. It was linear in plan (0.80 m wide x 0.28 m deep) with a rounded bowl-shaped profile and silty clay fills. Its upper fills were clearly cut by the adjacent ditch 3205. Ditch 3563 ran to the south-east for 19.5 m before being entirely cut away by ditch 3562.

Ditch 3432

Feature 3432 (0.60 m wide x 0.17m deep) was a badly truncated section of linear ditch on the same alignment as middle Iron Age enclosure ditch 3561. The feature had a flattened U-shaped profile. It clearly cut the Iron Age ditch and was itself largely cut away by the later ditch 3564. Just over 2.75 m of 3432 was visible in plan.

Earlier 2nd century AD *(Fig. 2.5)*

Ditch 3205

Feature 3205 was a relatively broad, flat bottomed ditch oriented north-east - south-west (*c* 2 m wide x 0.34 m deep). Clearly defined on the northern edge of site, the ditch was visible for a length of *c* 13.5 m before being lost in a series of later cuts and recuts of the trackway ditch (3562). The ditch appeared to branch into a T-shape at this point, one arm continuing towards the south-west, the other running off at right-angles towards the east where it formed the boundary between two fields.

Ditch 3564

Ditch 3564 defined the western half of the trackway during this period. It had a flattened bottom with straight sides (1.00–1.70 m wide x 0.40 m deep) and was recut on one occasion (3565). The ditch was visible for *c* 37 m stretching from the southern edge of the trench to within 3 m of the northern baulk. At its northern end it turned sharply to the west before being truncated by a series of later gullies (3568). The ditch contained pottery dated to the 2nd century AD and has been ascribed an early 2nd century date on the basis of its relationship with gully complex 3568, which is stratigraphically later, and its similarity in plan and dimensions to ditch 3205.

Ditch 3566

Ditch 3566 (0.80 m wide x *c* 0.30 m deep) was located 3 m to the west of, and roughly parallel to, 3205. The ditch contained 2nd century AD pottery and has been ascribed to the earlier part of that century on the basis of its stratigraphic relationship with the later ditch 3562. It is uncertain if 3566 and 3205 were contemporary.

Ditch 3567

This feature (*c* 1.5 m wide x 0.50 m deep) was almost totally obscured by a series of later gullies (3568) ascribed to the later 2nd century which cut into its upper fills. As a result it was only recognised in section as it ran beneath the north-western baulk of the trench. Although the ditch was fairly substantial and might have formed a field boundary similar to the north-eastern arm of 3205, no ceramic dating evidence was recovered and its position within this phase should be viewed as somewhat speculative.

Metalled surface 3532

Towards the southern end of the trackway a series of three shallow wheel ruts (3540, 3542 and 3545) were sealed beneath an irregular patch of corralian limestone blocks and cobbling which formed a metalled surface (3532). The metalling marked the centre of the trackway between the ditches 3205 and 3564 and was held within a fine matrix of sandy silt containing pottery dated to the 2nd century AD. The original extent of the cobbling is unclear but it seems likely that only the wetter areas were infilled with stone.

Later 2nd century AD *(Fig. 2.5)*

Feature 3562 (ditches 3235 and 3550)

Feature 3562 (*c* 1.30 m wide x 0.40 m deep) was part of a series of ditches which defined the eastern edge of the Roman track-way. It consisted of two separate recuts of the earlier ditch 3205. The recuts did not run the entire length of 3205 but only along its southern half, turning towards the east at its midpoint to scour the eastern arm of the field ditch. Ditch 3562 clearly truncated the earlier ditch 3566 and the metalled road surface 3532.

Gully complex 3568

This feature comprised a complex of three or four intercutting gullies all of which ran from the north-west to the south-east, cutting ditch 3564 and the upper fills of ditch 3567. The precise sequence of gullies could not be determined. The orientation of the complex suggests that the gullies may have cut directly across the Roman trackway to the north of the trench. It is more probable, however, that they turned sharply to the north-west to follow the alignment of the trackway.

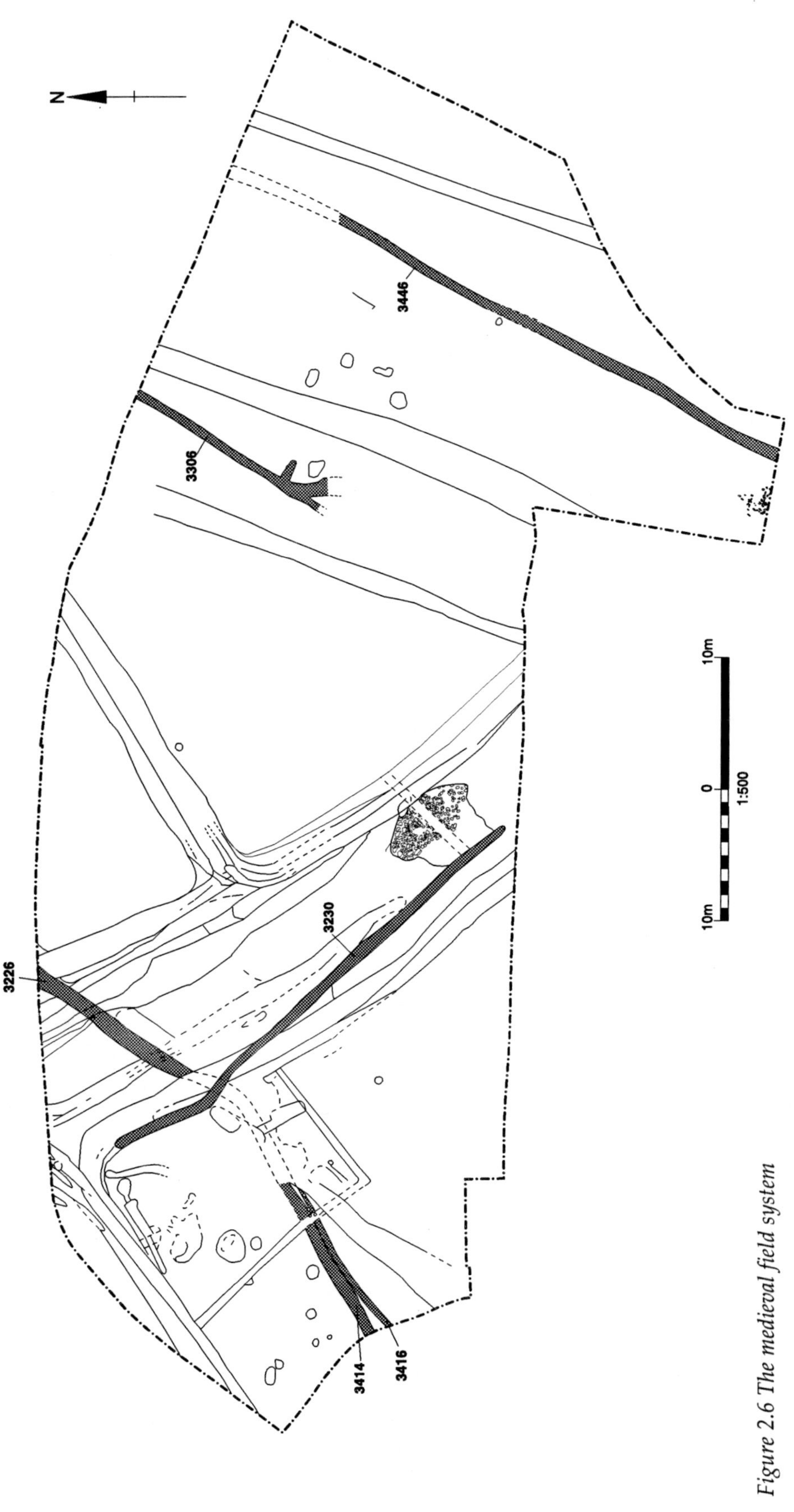

Figure 2.6 The medieval field system

The medieval period *(Fig. 2.6)*

A number of largely undated linear features making up a coherent field system were ascribed to the medieval period on the basis of a minimal amount of pottery and their stratigraphically later relationship with the Roman archaeology. Although the features were very heavily truncated and only a few sherds of medieval pottery were recovered, part of the field system cut obliquely across the Roman trackway and was demonstrably the most recent archaeology in the trench.

Ditch 3230

Although the detail of individual fields had altered since the Roman period, the alignment of 3230 (0.90 m wide x 0.40 m deep) suggests some degree of overall continuity in the structure of the landscape. Although the ditch closely follows the alignment of the Roman trackway, it clearly cut all of the Roman features it crossed and contained sherds of medieval pottery. The ditch was first visible *c* 5 m from the northern edge of excavation. From there it was traced for *c* 40 m towards the south-east before terminating just short of the south-western edge of the trench. The ditch had a distinctive kink in its alignment towards its northern end, marking the intersection with a second ditch (3226).

Ditch 3226

Although very heavily truncated, this linear feature (1.50 m wide x 0.17 m deep) also contained a small amount of medieval pottery. The ditch cut obliquely across the alignment of the Roman trackway on a north-east - south-west orientation. Because of the shallow nature of the ditch it is unclear whether its south-western end connected directly with 3230 or stopped short of it. Whatever the case, the ditch was clearly aligned on the point where 3230 kinked, marking the corner of four separate fields.

Ditch 3414

A third ditch 3414 (*c* 1 m wide x 0.22 m deep), oriented on an alignment similar to 3226 on the western side of 3230, completed the cruciform pattern of field ditches. The ditch was of a character very similar to 3226 and was also extremely heavily truncated. A shallow gully 3416 (0.30 - 0.40 m wide x 0.06 m deep) was located immediately adjacent and parallel to 3414 on its southern side. The gully was visible for 9 m before being obscured by a modern drainage feature.

Ditches 3306 and 3446

Ditches 3306 and 3446 were located in the otherwise archaeologically sterile south eastern corner of the trench. The ditches were parallel and oriented south-west - north-east. Both were relatively shallow (*c* 0.70 – 0.80 m wide x 0.18 m deep) and 3306 petered out at its south-western end. Just before that point a small spur of soil suggests that a cross ditch may have once linked 3306 and 3446 together. The phasing of the two ditches must remain uncertain since neither produced any dating evidence. On balance, however, it is likely that they were medieval in date given their coherent spatial relationship with other medieval features and similarity of depth and character.

Undated features

A series of three linear ditches crossed the south-eastern end of the trench. The ditches were on a similar alignment and were thought to be of a broadly similar date. Only one of the features was excavated and this proved to be shallow. The features were not aligned with the rest of the Roman archaeology and, although one ditch (3207) contained a Roman knife blade, it is more likely that the features were later in date, possibly medieval or post-medieval.

TRENCH 33 *(Fig. 2.7)*

The earlier prehistoric period *(Fig. 2.8)*

The earlier prehistoric phase is represented almost entirely by redeposited artefactual evidence recovered from Iron Age features. Evidence for earlier prehistoric negative features is meagre and confined to two lengths of linear ditch 5961 and 6305.

Ditch 5961

Ditch 5961 was located near to the centre of the southern baulk of Trench 33. It was linear in plan and projected 4.10 m from the baulk in a north-westerly direction. It ended in a rounded terminal. The ditch was 0.75 m wide x 0.20 m deep and was filled with an orangey brown deposit which was uncharacteristic of the fills over the rest of the trench. The ditch contained three sherds of earlier prehistoric pottery and was over-lain by two circular structures (5087 and 5257) dated to the early/ middle Iron Age (see Fig. 2.10).

Ditch 6305

Ditch 6305 (=6304) was located 6.5 m to the south-west of 5961. It was linear, though slightly sinuous in plan with a bowl-shaped profile. It had a variable width measuring 0.80–1.10 m wide and was 0.40 m deep. The ditch was oriented north-west - south-east and first appeared *c* 4 m from the south-eastern baulk of the trench where it was partly obscured by modern disturbance. From that point it ran for 21 m towards the north-west where it was cut away by the Roman ditch 5359. Ditch 6305 contained no dating evidence but was cut in a number of places by the middle Iron Age structure 5021 and by the Roman ditch 5359. Its dating remains uncertain but it shared some characteristics with ditch 5961 including its form, the unusual orangey brown fill and a common orientation.

It is unlikely to be a coincidence that spatial analysis of redeposited earlier prehistoric artefacts identified a concentration of pre-Iron Age flint to the west of these features which corresponds to the distribution of Bronze Age pottery (Fig. 2.8).

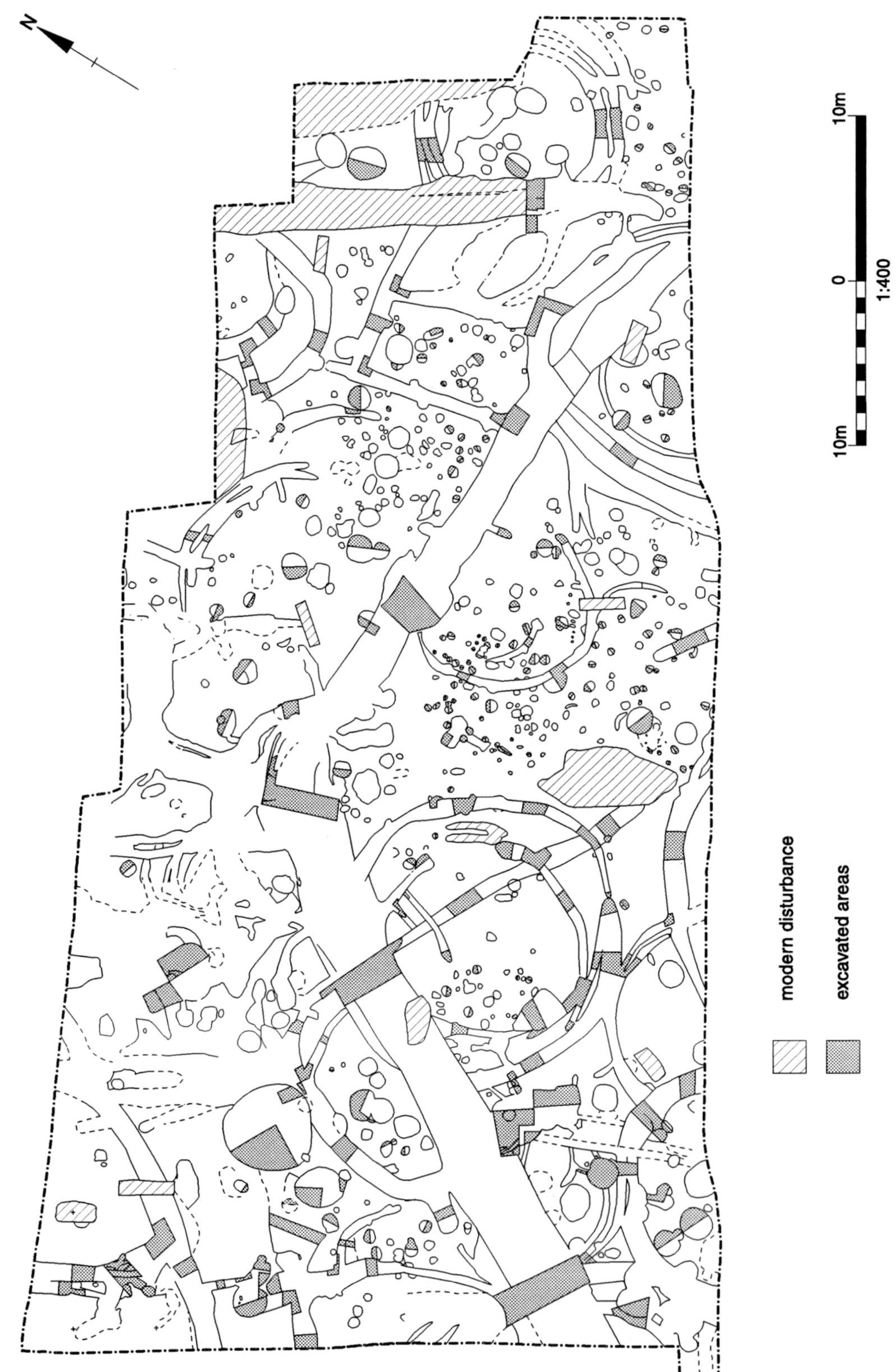

Figure 2.7 Trench 33, all periods

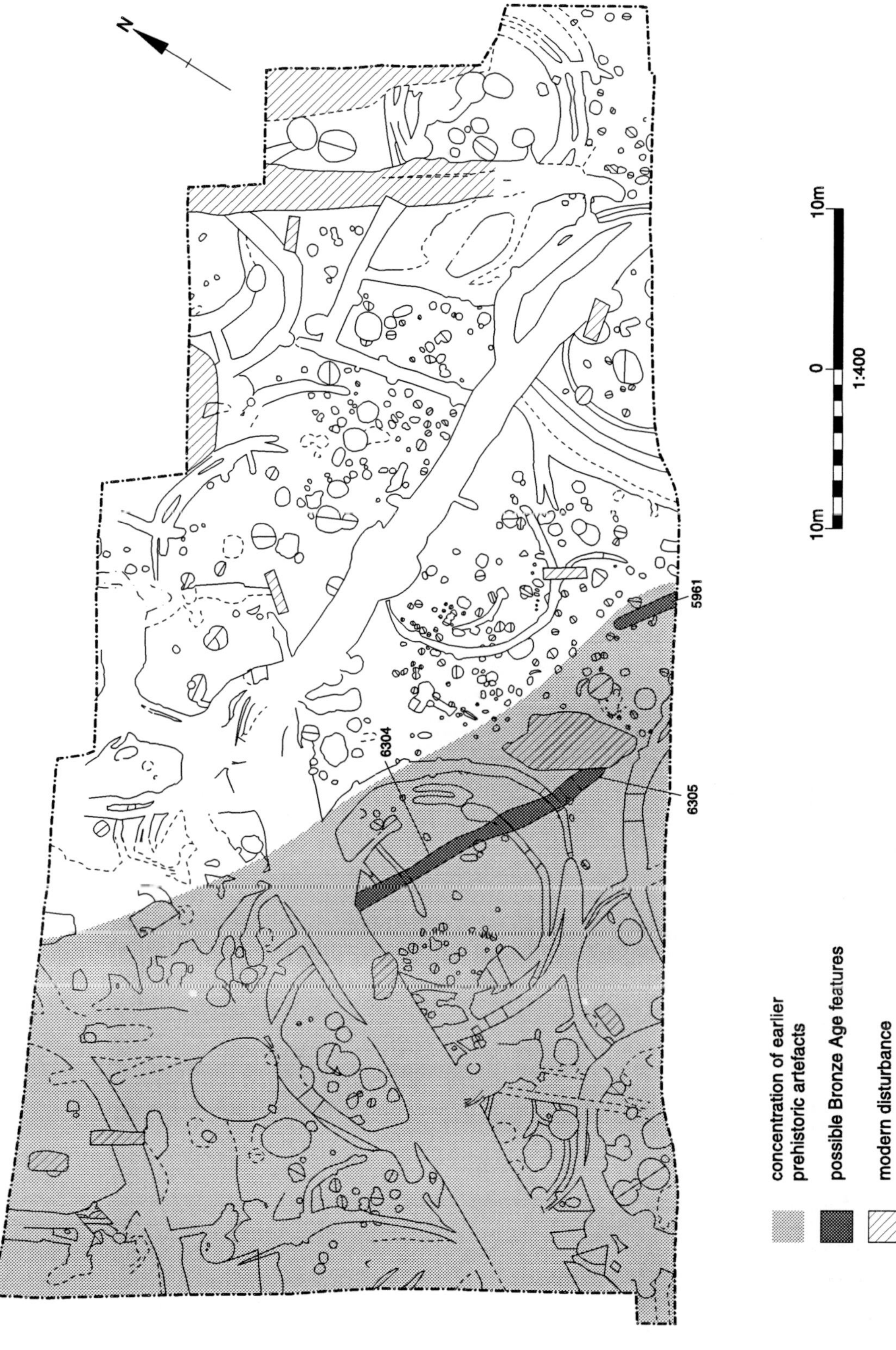

Figure 2.8 Earlier prehistoric activity (Trench 33)

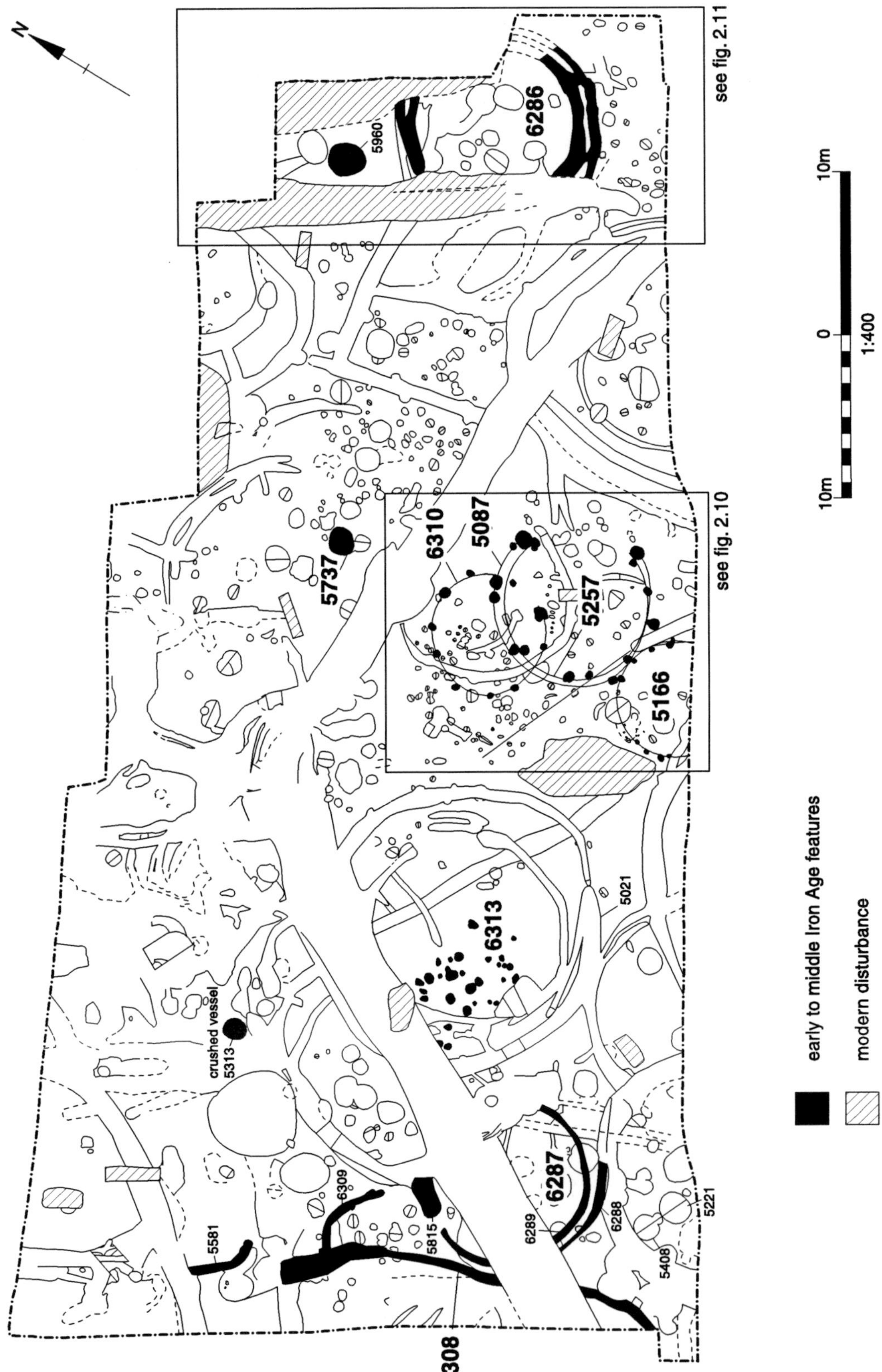

Figure 2.9 Early to middle Iron Age activity (Trench 33)

The early to middle Iron Age *(Fig. 2.9)*

Possible post-built circular structures

A number of post-built structures have been postulated partly on the basis of ceramic evidence and partly on the basis of spatial analysis. It is stressed that the structures described are only one possible interpretation extrapolated from a mass of largely undated postholes (see below). The interpretation of these structures is discussed in Chapter 5.

Structures 5257 and 5087 *(Figs 2.9 and 2.10)*

Structures 5257 and 5087 are probably two phases - the building and sub-sequent rebuilding - of a roundhouse or circular structure on the same site. During the rebuilding (5087) the wall line and postholes were shifted very slightly outward presumably to avoid the ground disturbed by the earlier building 5257.

Structure 5257 consisted of seven postholes which formed a circle with a diameter of 8.5 m. Although the postholes were all filled with a dark grey sandy silt, they ranged widely in diameter (0.14–0.48 m) and especially in depth (0.05–0.42 m). The postholes formed a regular circle, however, and the width and depth of postholes need be no more than a reflection of the available timber. Only two sherds of pottery were recovered from the structure: a single sherd of decorated beaker from posthole 5226 (which is thought to be redeposited) and a sherd of early Iron Age pottery from posthole 5168.

Structure 5087 consisted of six well-spaced postholes forming a circle with a diameter of *c* 9 m. The postholes were extremely consistent in both depth and diameter, and were filled with the same dark grey sandy silt throughout. Three of the postholes contained pottery dated to the early or early/middle Iron Age (5088, 5102 and 5110). Posthole 5102 was partially cut away by posthole 5100 which contained a single sherd of middle Iron Age pottery. The eastern side of the structure was marked by a 6 m wide entrance gap between two substantial postholes 5088 and 5110. Although unusually wide for a roundhouse entrance, this arrangement mirrored the entrance structure of the earlier building 5257.

Structure 5166 *(Figs 2.9 and 2.10)*

Although partially obscured by the south-eastern edge of the excavation, the projected extent of structure 5166 would give an approximate diameter of 7 m. Seven postholes were revealed within the excavation area, each with a diameter ranging between 0.25 m and 0.30 m. The post circle was broken to the west by a circular pit (5270) which contained middle Iron Age pottery. A second pit which was revealed within the post circle may have been associated with the structure but was not excavated. The three postholes which were excavated within the post circle contained no dating evidence and are of uncertain phase. The dating of the structure itself is similarly uncertain as five of the postholes contained ceramics ranging from the early to middle Iron Age in date. Despite these difficulties, however, the structure forms a coherent circle of well-matched postholes containing a dark grey sandy silt.

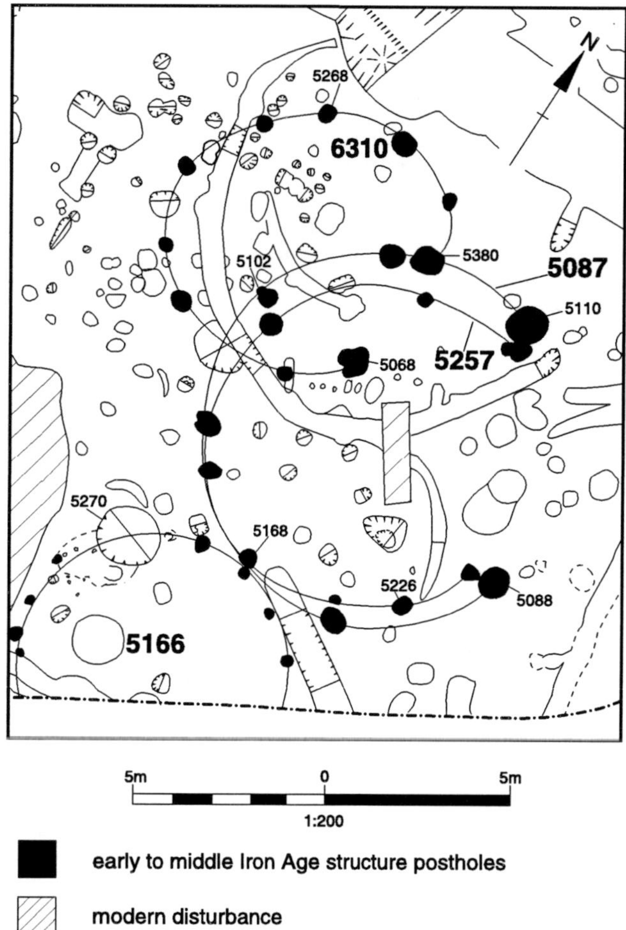

Figure 2.10 Early to middle Iron Age post-built structures

Structure 6310 *(Figs 2.9 and 2.10)*

Structure 6310 was approximately circular with a diameter of 7 m. It consisted of ten postholes ranging in diameter from 0.30 to 0.55 m which contained mid-grey sandy silt. The two largest postholes (5068 and 5380) marked the doorposts of an east-facing entrance *c* 3 m wide. Of the two, only posthole 5068 was excavated and was found to have been recut on at least two occasions. The excavated posthole contained limestone post-packing and clear evidence of a postpipe. Ceramics from two of the postholes (5068 and 5268) suggest that the structure may date from the early/middle Iron Age. There were many possibly contemporary postholes within the interior of the structure, two of which (5102 and 5446) did contain pottery of the same period. Overall, the structure was extremely convincing. The circle of postholes formed a good, coherent plan and the east-facing aspect of the entrance is a common feature of roundhouses in the region (Hingley and Miles 1984, 63).

Other post-built structures

Structure 6313 *(Fig. 2.9)*

Structure 6313 consisted of a discreet group of postholes within the western half of Structure 5021. The postholes were mostly subcircular but of widely varying profiles and dimensions. Pottery was recovered from three of the postholes and ranged in date from the early to middle Iron Age. Although the postholes formed a discreet group, no obvious structure was discernible. A number of the postholes were clearly cut by structure 5021 and it is probable that the posthole cluster represents an earlier post-built structure or structures.

Ditched circular structures

Structure 6286 *(Fig. 2.11)*

Structure 6286 was located on the eastern edge of Trench 33. The north-eastern quadrant of the structure lay outside of the trench and its western half had been truncated by modern disturbance, leaving only a central area of the structure undamaged. It consisted of a series of concentric gullies representing at least three phases of activity.

The first phase, dating from the early to middle Iron Age, is represented by gullies 6050 and 6183. Because the plan of the structure was incomplete it was impossible to definitively match the northern and southern sequence of gullies. On the basis of morphological similarities it is suggested that gullies 6050 and 6183 were part of the same circle. If so, the ring gully would have had an internal diameter of 10.5 m, a dimension which is entirely consistent with other ring gullies on the site. The two gullies had similar depths and profiles with relatively steep, almost vertical sides and narrow, flat bases. There was no sign of a break in either gully but an entrance could easily have been obscured under the side of the trench to the east or cut away by the modern truncation to the west.

The second phase, dating to the middle Iron Age, is represented by gullies 6048 and 6139. Although their profiles were slightly different, 6048 and 6139 may well have been part of the same ring gully. Gully 6048 had a slightly flattened bottom with straight sides sloping at *c* 50–60°. Gully 6139 had a steep, near vertical edge on its external side (0.50 m deep) and a stepped profile on its inside edge. The deep and narrow shape of its profile (Fig. 2.12) suggests that it may have held the uprights of a roundhouse wall rather than have acted as a drip gully (see Chapter 5).

Gully 6046, belonging to the third phase, was of a later, middle Iron Age date. Its character was quite different to any of the other gullies comprising structure 6286, and it is possible that it was not part of the structure at all or that it reflected an addition or repair to an established roundhouse. The gully was quite shallow (0.12 m) with a gently rounded bottom and was present only on the northern half of the structure.

A number of pits were revealed in the vicinity of structure 6286. Immediately to the north-east of the structure was a large circular pit 5960 (Fig. 2.11). The pit contained early - middle Iron Age pottery and may have been contemporary with the earlier phases of structure 6286. A group of pits of varying sizes were revealed within the circular structure. Only one of these (5817) was excavated and contained middle Iron Age pottery. As structure 6286 was constructed in the early – middle Iron Age and then underwent alterations and rebuilding over an extended period, it is possible that the pit was an internal feature of the latest phase of the roundhouse.

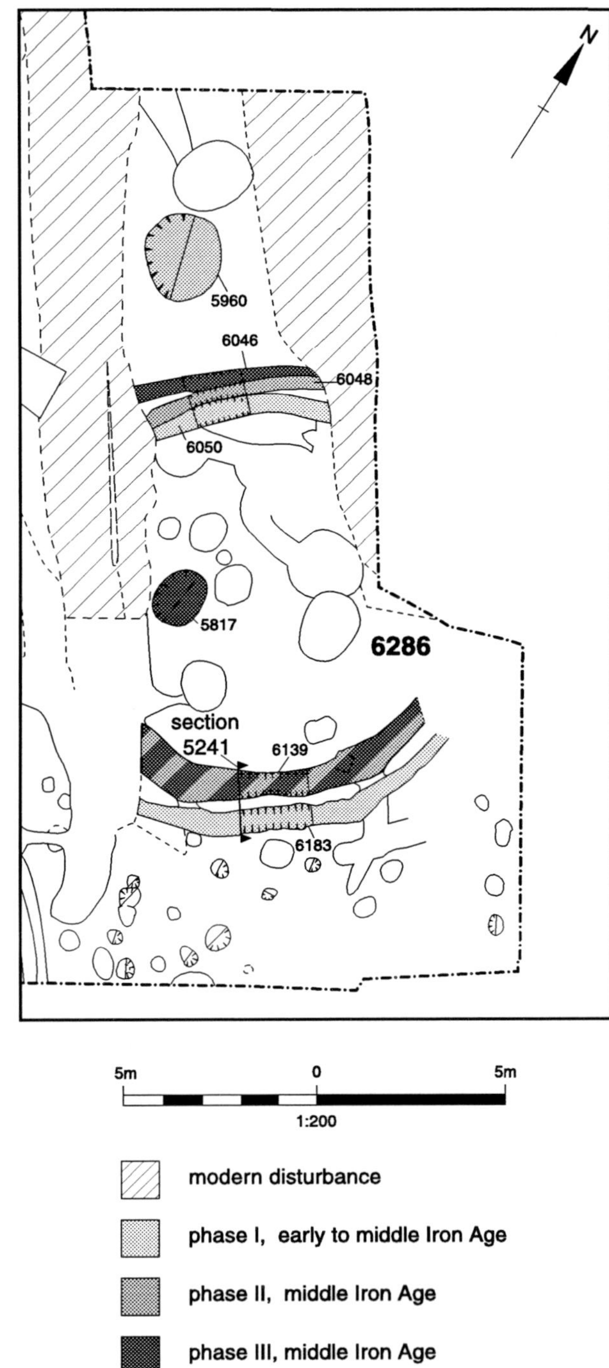

Figure 2.11 Structure 6286

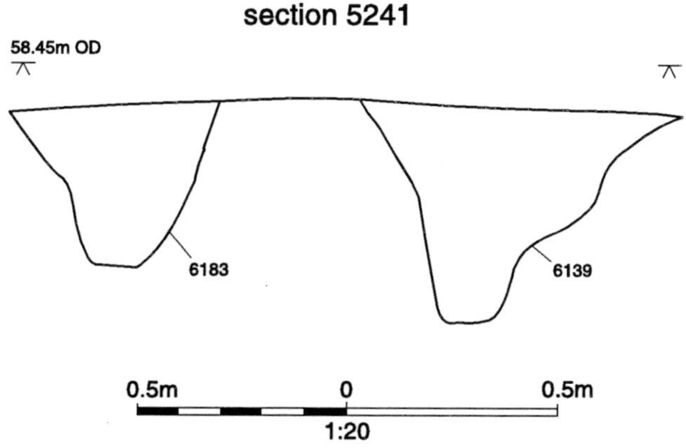

Figure 2.12 Gully profiles, structure 6286

Structure 6287 *(Fig. 2.9)*

Structure 6287 was located near to the southern corner of Trench 33 immediately to the south-west of structure 5021. It consisted of a double ring gully (6289 and 6228) with a possible north-west facing entrance.

The eastern edge of ring gully 6289 was largely obliterated by later pits and a Roman ditch (5359) which ran through its centre. Enough survived, however, to project an estimated diameter of *c* 10 m. The gully had a shallow profile (0.12 m deep x 0.38 m wide).

Ring-gully 6288 lay immediately to the south of 6289 and followed its arc very closely. One of the gullies (it is unclear which) appeared to the north-west of the Roman ditch 5359 where it terminated, possibly forming a north-west facing entrance. The width of the entrance is uncertain since one of the terminals was obscured by the later ditch 5815.

A number of pits and postholes were located in the vicinity of 6287. The majority, however, were either not excavated or contained no dating evidence. Only one pit (5408) could be safely dated to the early middle Iron Age. It contained ceramics of that date and cut through an early Iron Age posthole (5409).

Other features

Ditches 6308 and 6309 *(Fig. 2.9)*

Feature 6308 was located immediately to the west of 6287. It consisted of a slightly sinuous gully (0.20 m wide x 0.40 m deep) which emerged from an area of soil marks in the southern corner of Trench 33. It was visible for *c* 24 m towards the north-west, apparently curving around 6287 before widening to 1.5 m. At that point the gully was truncated by pit 5641. A gully (5581) of the original, narrower width appeared on the other side of this pit, going on to connect with the possible boundary ditch 6298. It is uncertain whether that gully was the continuation of 6308 or if there was an entrance gap destroyed by 5641. It is possible that 6308 was the same gully as 6288 in which case the gully would have partially enclosed structure 6287.

Gully 6309 was a curved, narrow gully projecting from 6308 for 5.5 m towards the east. If contemporary, its position to the north-west of structure 6287 would have effectively demarcated a small 'yard' or working area in front of the entrance to 6287. Its dimensions and curved form were similar to 5581 suggesting that the two gullies were contemporary and part of the same barrier or fence-line (6308).

A number of isolated postholes and pits were ascribed to this period on the basis of their ceramic content (Fig. 2.9). One of these features contained a crushed pottery vessel dated to the early Iron Age. It is probable that other small pits and postholes containing no dateable artefacts were also of this date.

The middle Iron Age *(Fig. 2.13)*

The roundhouses

Middle Iron Age activity on the site was characterised by a series of single and multiphase ring gullies which marked the sites of roundhouses. The most impressive of these was the large double-ringed structure 5021 located near to the centre of Trench 33.

Structure 5021 *(Fig. 2.14)*

Structure 5021 consisted of a series of penannular gullies together forming a circular double ring within which there was evidence of internal divisions. The structure overlay an earlier ditch (6304=6305) and was cut away on its north-western side by the Roman boundary ditch 5359. A group of postholes clustered within the south-western quadrant of the structure was not believed to be associated with the developed 5021 but may have formed an earlier post-built structure (6313) which occupied the same site (see above). The development of the gullies forming structure 5021 may be divided into two major phases, the first represented by gullies 5338 and 6281, and the second by gully 5339.

Curvilinear gully 5338 belongs to the earliest of the two major phases of ring gullies. Although cut away at its northern end by the Roman ditch 5359 and in the south by the penannular gully 5339, a substantial part of its eastern side survived. The feature was widest in the north-east (0.90 m) but gradually narrowed to 0.30 m in the south where it was truncated by the more substantial ditch 5339. Just over 5 m to the west of that point, a narrow, 3 m long slot (5342), which had the same profile and depth (0.08 m) as 5338, was believed to be its continuation. If so, the ring gully would have had a diameter of *c* 14 m. The slot ended in a pointed terminal which marked the southern end of a possible west-facing entrance. A small pointed featured (6314) largely destroyed by the Roman ditch 5359 was believed to be the northern terminal, demarcating a 4 m wide entrance.

Gully 6281 was located between the inner and outer rings of structure 5021. It was approximately 8 m in length and had a flat bottom with relatively steep sides. The relationship between its eastern terminal and ditch

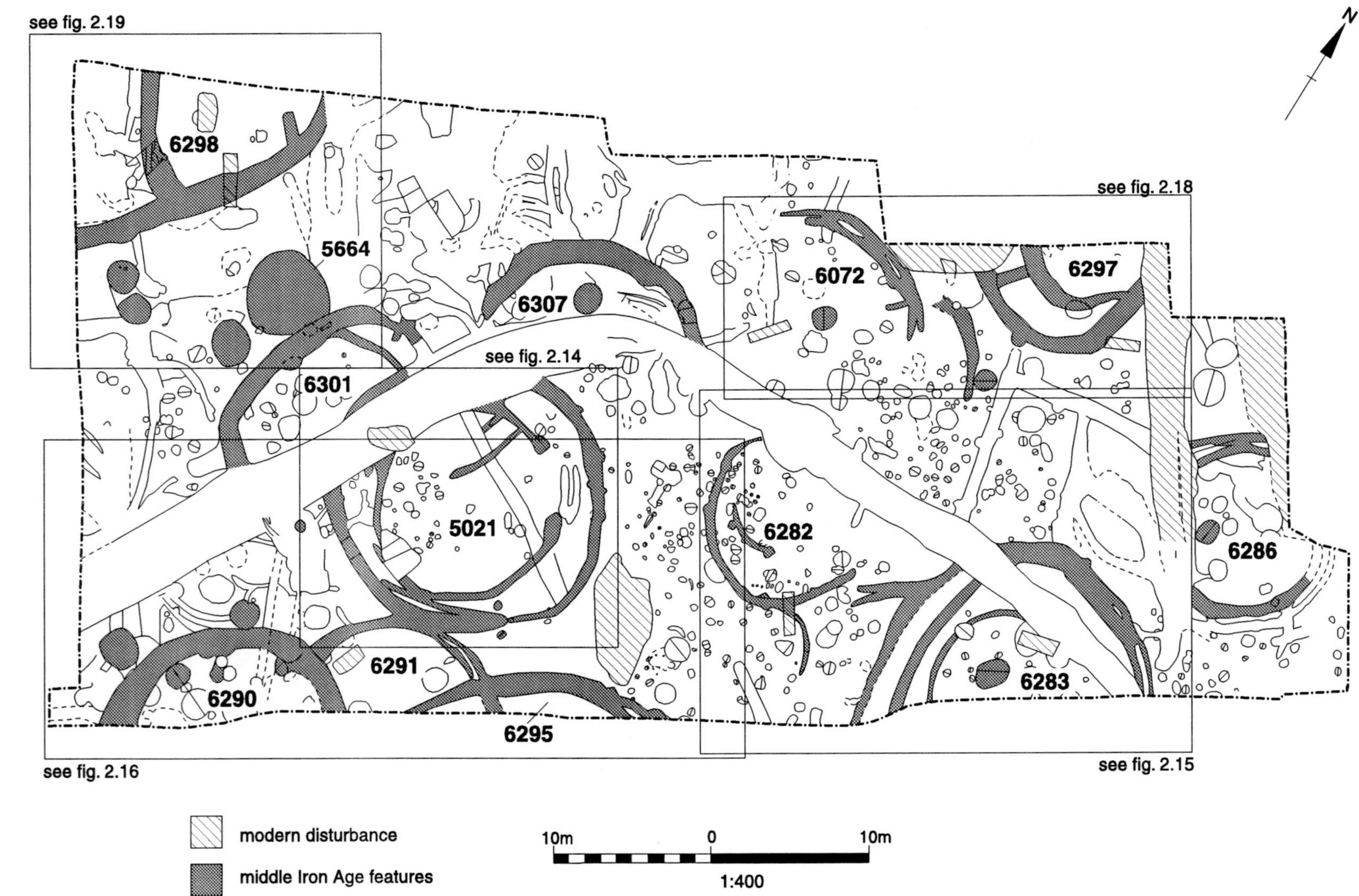

Figure 2.13 Middle Iron Age activity (Trench 33)

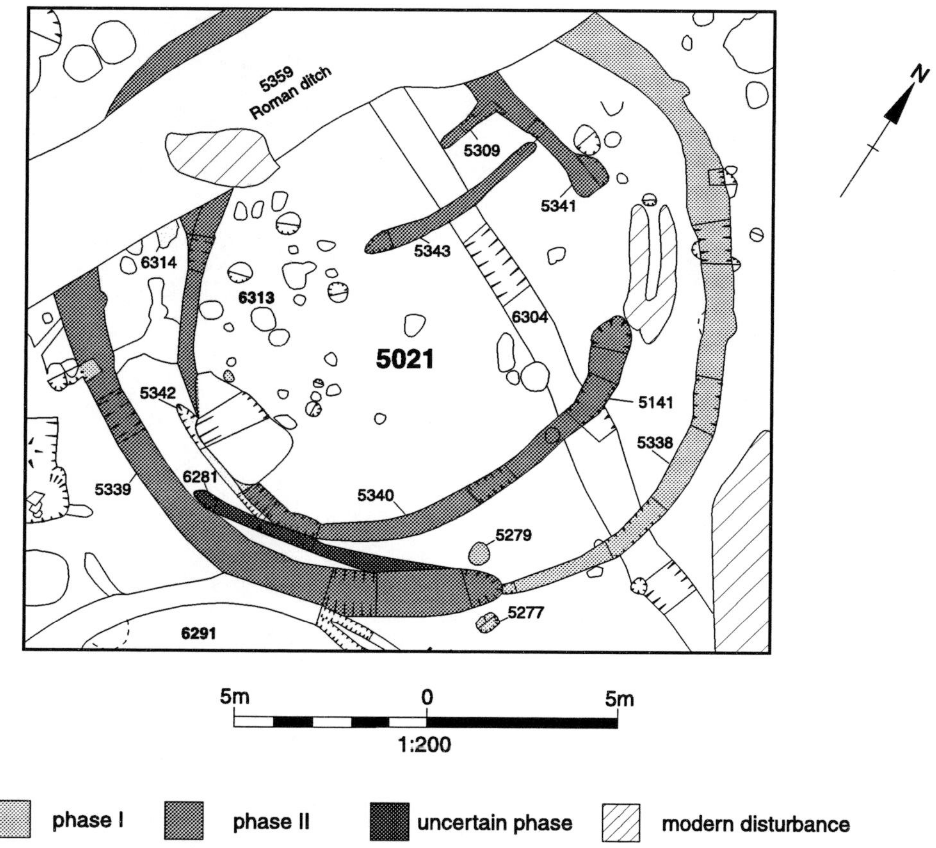

Figure 2.14 Structure 5021

5339 was unclear. Similarly, the relationship between 6281 and 5338 was not determined though it is possible that 6281 was a recut of 5338 which would have widened the entrance to 6.5 m.

In the second phase, the southern half of the outer ring of structure 5021 was defined by the curvilinear gully 5339. This feature terminated midway along the southern half of the outer ring where it clearly cut 5338. At its northern end it was itself cut away by the Roman ditch 5359. It is possible that postholes 5277 and 5279, which were located at either side of the terminal, were associated with 5339. One of the postholes (5277) contained two sherds of pottery dated to the early and early/middle Iron Age respectively. Posthole 5279 contained a single sherd of decorated Beaker pottery which was thought to be redeposited.

Gully 5340/5341 formed the inner ring of structure 5021. The feature was oval in plan (13 x 11 m) and had a uniform depth of 0.28 m. It had a U-shaped profile and a flattened bottom. In the north-eastern quadrant a 3.5 m wide entrance was demarcated by two terminals. The terminals were slightly bulbous in plan and contained a significant quantity of burnt limestone which may have been used as postpacking. Whether the gully functioned as a wall-slot or drip-gully remains uncertain (see Chapter 5).

To the north and west of the ring gully entrance, a pair of linear slots, 5309 and 5343, partially traversed the roundhouse interior. Both slots were approximately 0.40 m wide with flat bottoms and relatively steep sides. The longer of the two (5343) was 5.5 m in length and curved slightly away from the entrance. Unlike 5309 which was *c* 1.75 m long, the slot did not connect with the ring gully 5341 but stopped some 0.10 m short. The function of the twin slots is uncertain and is discussed further below.

Structure 6282 *(Fig. 2.15)*

Structure 6282 was located to the east of structure 5021. It consisted of a penannular gully with an east-facing entrance and a curvilinear gully which defined a possible annex.

Penannular gully 5337 defined a sub-circular area approximately 10.5 m in diameter. A 2.5 m wide entrance was located between the terminals 6255 and 6257 on the south-eastern side of the structure. The gully had a uniform width of *c* 0.50 m except in its north-west quadrant where it narrowed to a point before being cut away by the Roman boundary ditch 5359. It is unclear whether the narrowing of the ditch indicated the existence of a second entranceway (see Chapter 5). Five segments were excavated across the feature including both terminals.

A second, short length of gully (5029) was revealed within the western half of the ring gully interior. This

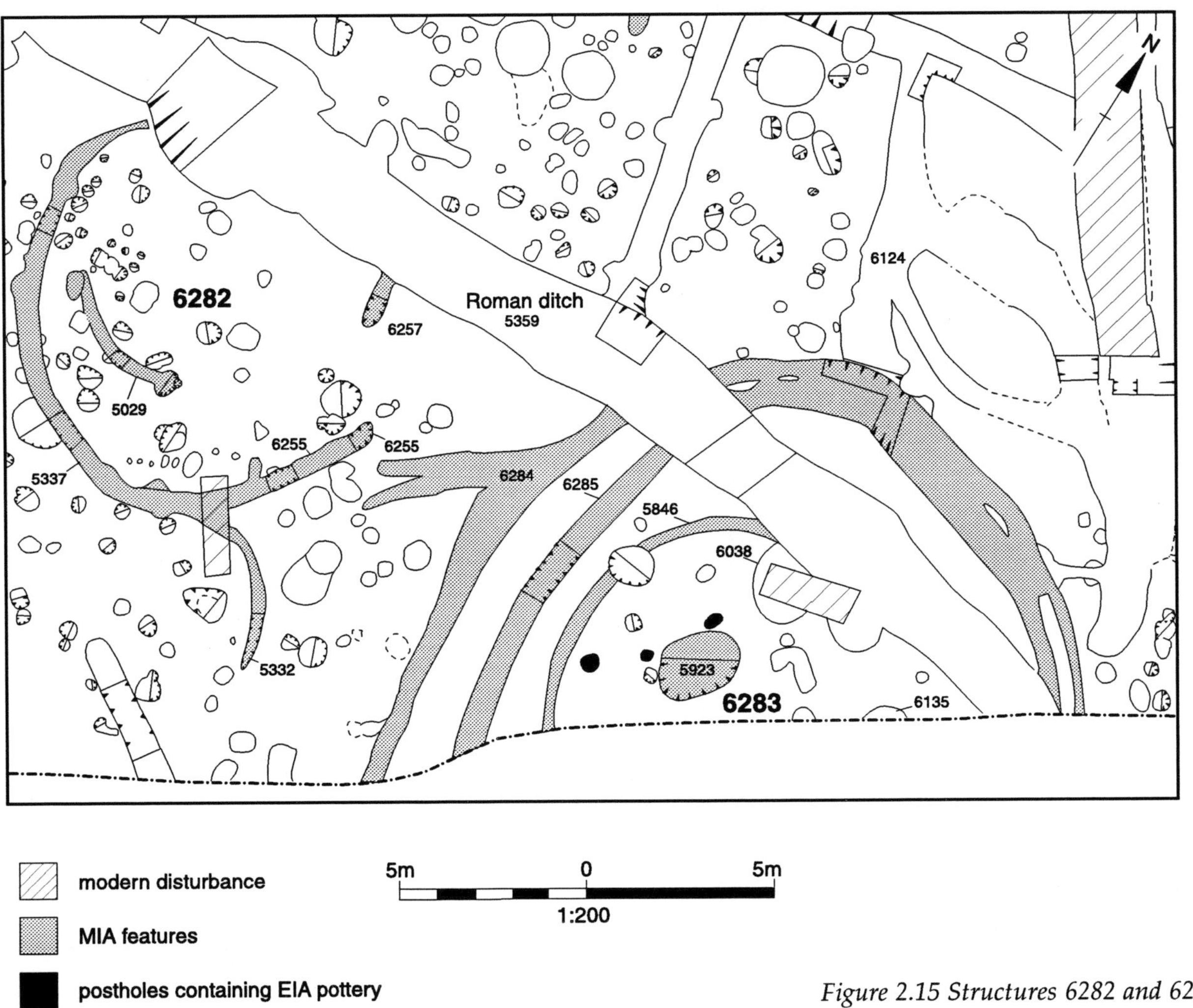

Figure 2.15 Structures 6282 and 6283

feature was slightly curved and may be associated with a pair of postholes which were located at either end of it. Only one of the postholes (5026) was excavated, however, and it contained no dating evidence.

A short length of curvilinear gully (5332) protruded from the southern side of 5337. The gully curved away from the main enclosure before terminating at a blunt point. If projected as a circle the gully would have had an approximate diameter of 5 m. No corresponding length of gully was found to the west, however, and it must be assumed that the gully was never penannular or circular.

Structure 6282 was located in an area of dense postholes. The majority of these postholes were not excavated, however, and no obvious post-built structures, which may have been contemporary with 6282, could be identified. A number of the postholes have been ascribed to earlier post-built structures 5087, 5257, 6310 and 5166 (see above). The great majority of postholes remain unattributed to any structure.

Structure 6283 *(Fig. 2.15)*

Structure 6283 was located on the south-eastern edge of Trench 33 to the east of structure 6282. It consisted of a ring gully within a double-ditched enclosure and possibly associated pits and postholes.

Approximately one half to two thirds of ring gully 5846 lay within the excavation area. The eastern half of the structure had been heavily truncated by the Roman boundary ditch 5359. The western half consisted of a curving gully *c* 9 m in length. Based upon the projected extent of the gully, the complete structure would have been approximately 10 m in diameter. Where excavated the gully was relatively wide (*c* 0.40 m) compared to its depth (*c* 0.08 m) suggesting a considerable degree of truncation. It is probable that the gully functioned either as a construction trench for a post-built roundhouse or as its drip gully. Given the degree of truncation, however, further speculation concerning function would be of limited value.

The absence of an eastern return to the ring gully (in an area which was not truncated by the Roman boundary ditch) suggests the structure may have had an east-facing entrance. If so, this would be consistent with the widely recognised pattern of round-house orientation both in the Upper Thames Valley (Hingley and Miles 1984, 63) and elsewhere (Oswald 1997, 87–88).

Ditch 6285 was the inner of two apparently continuous ditches surrounding ring gully 5846. The ditch enclosed an oval or subcircular area of 9 x 16.5 m and had a gentle, U-shaped profile with a rounded bottom and variable depth (0.22–0.30 m) and width (0.40–0.70 m).

Ditch 6284 lay immediately outside of 6285 and was very similar in plan, enclosing an area 9.75 x 18.5 m. One section was excavated through 6284 in order to investigate its relationship with the north-south ditch 6124. Ditch 6284 was not visible in the section, however, and was assumed to have been completely cut away by 6124. The relationship between 6284 and 6285 could not be established with any certainty.

A double ditched spur or annex extended from the western side of 6284. The feature was unexcavated but its orientation and length suggest a possible spatial relationship with the doorway of adjacent structure 6282.

A number of pits and postholes of varying dimensions were revealed within the area of structure 6283 (posthole cluster 6316). It was clear from the stratigraphic relationships that not all of the pits could have been contemporary with the ring gully 5846.

Although no coherent structure could be formed from the pattern of postholes or from the analysis of their fills and dimensions, three of the postholes contained early Iron Age pottery and a fourth, which contained two middle Iron Age sherds, had a noticeably different fill from the others. This would suggest that some of the posts were contemporary with each other and may have formed an earlier post-built structure. Not all of the postholes were excavated.

The phasing of structure 6283 presents a number of problems. Where ceramic evidence was recovered it was in small quantities and the degree of redeposition is uncertain. Although set within a possible middle Iron Age enclosure (6285), no dating evidence was recovered from the ring gully and there was no direct evidence that the two were contemporary. The ring gully itself was truncated by a pit containing two sherds of early Iron Age pottery, which were presumably redeposited.

The clustering of pits within 6283 is unlikely to have been coincidental (5923, 6038 and 6135). Two of these three pits remained unexcavated, however, and, in the absence of a stratigraphic sequence, phasing is difficult. The third pit contained middle Iron Age pottery and may have been an internal feature of the roundhouse defined by ring gully 5846.

Structure 6286

The middle Iron Age phase of 6286 is described with the early to middle Iron Age phase of this structure above.

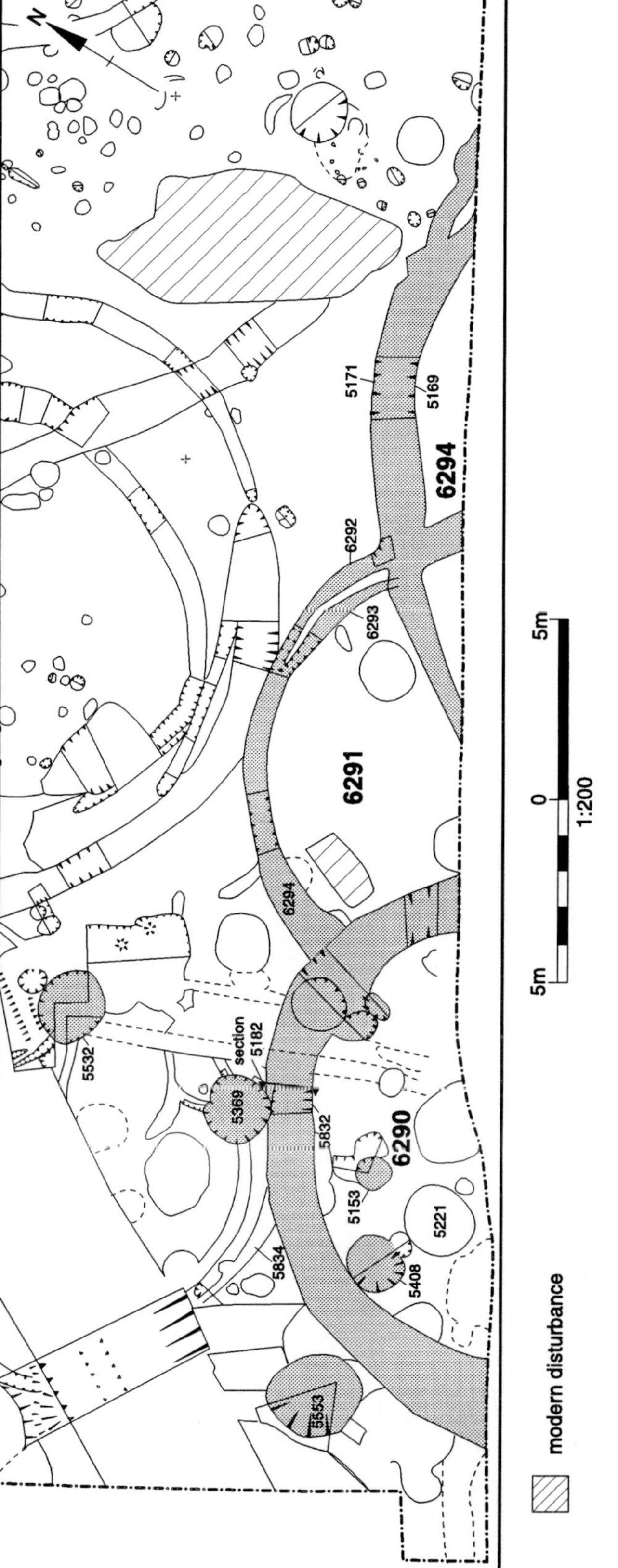

Figure 2.16 Structures 6290, 6291 and 6295 and middle Iron Age pits

Structure 6290 (Fig. 2.16)

Structure 6290 was located in the south-western corner of Trench 33. Due to an inadequate level of excavation the structure was not clearly understood in the field and interpretation is subsequently limited. However, the feature contained enough middle Iron Age pottery to date it securely to that period. The feature appears to have consisted of a U-shaped curvilinear ditch (5832) with an average depth of 0.34 m. The ditch only partially fell within the excavated area and although it is impossible to reconstruct its plan with certainty, it is probable, given the nature of the site, that the structure would have been approximately circular with an estimated diameter of 13 m. It is clear from section 5182 (Fig. 2.17) that although the structure had no stratigraphic relationship with the early/middle Iron Age structure 6287 it did cut another feature (5839). Section 5182 is the only evidence for the existence of 5839, and as no further investigation was carried out, it is impossible to be certain whether the feature was an earlier ring gully or a pit. Early/ middle Iron Age pits did exist in the immediate vicinity of the section (5408 and 5221) but since 5839 was also cut by the early / middle Iron Age gully 5834 (structure 6287), the feature must be presumed to be earlier still.

A concentration of subcircular pits was revealed in the vicinity of structure 6290. Not all of these pits were excavated, but it is clear from stratigraphic evidence that not all of them could be contemporary with the structure. It is possible, however, that some or all of the pits were associated with structure 5021 to the north-east. If this was the case, then it might suggest that structure 5021 had become the dominant structure and that 6290 had been demolished and the area reused for underground storage.

Structure 6291 *(Fig. 2.16)*

Structure 6291 was located immediately to the north-east of structure 6290. It consisted of two curvilinear gullies 6292 and 6293 which, like structure 6290, were interrupted by the south-eastern baulk of the Trench. If projected as a circle the feature would have had an estimated diameter of 12 to 13 m. As the south-western end of the structure did not continue beyond Structure 6290 it would appear to have terminated at or within the junction between the two. Unfortunately, the relationship between the two structures was entirely destroyed by a complex sequence of inter-cutting pits which contained considerable amounts of middle Iron Age pottery. Similarly, all of the main components of 6291 appeared to date to the middle Iron Age.

Structure 6295 *(Fig. 2.16)*

Structure 6295 was located halfway along the south-eastern baulk of Trench 33 immediately to the north-east of structure 6291. It consisted of two curvilinear gullies (5169 and 5171) which ran close together except at their eastern end where they divided before running under the south-eastern baulk of the trench. Although superficially similar to 6291 and 6290, the structure did not have the same degree of curvature as the other two structures and may have functioned as an enclosure ditch (see Chapter 5). Although the field records note the possibility that 6295 was cut through by 6291, the relationship was very uncertain. As with 6290 and 6291 structure 6295 contained middle Iron Age pottery.

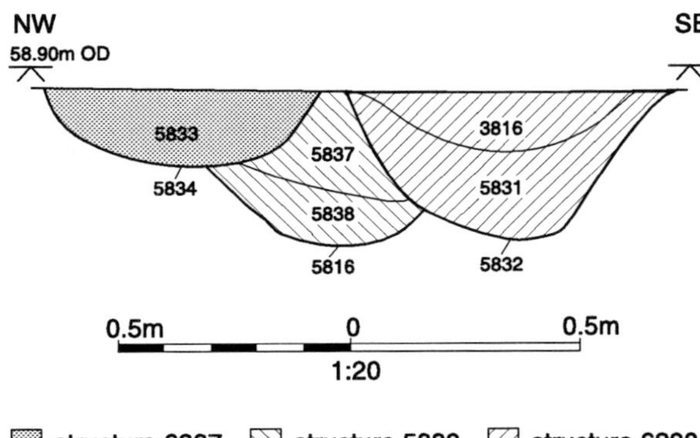

Figure 2.17 Section through gullies 5839 and 5316

Structure 6297 *(Fig. 2.18)*

Structure 6297 seems to have had three phases of construction. In phase one the structure consisted of a curvilinear gully (6149) with a U-shaped profile (0.50 m wide x 0.20 m deep). A second gully (6220) approached 6149 at right angles from the south-west but it is unclear whether the two gullies actually formed part of the same structure. Phase two of the structure saw a recutting and widening of 6149. Phase three involved the excavation of a second curvilinear ditch (6219) two metres to the south of 6149 which curved round to cut it in the north-east. Both the recut of 6149 and the new ditch (6219) cut through the linear ditch 6220.

Windbreak features

A number of features were located within Trench 33 which consisted of one or more curved gullies defining semicircular areas. Three certain examples were identified, usually located in the vicinity of pits or postholes. One possible function of these features may have been to protect open working areas from the wind. Without exception the features arched away from the north, perhaps indicating the direction of the prevailing wind.

Structures 6072, 6306 and 6307 *(Fig. 2.18)*

Structure 6072 was the best preserved example of the 'windbreak' type features. It consisted of two semi-circular gullies which ran parallel to each other over a distance of 12 m. Although curved, the feature was

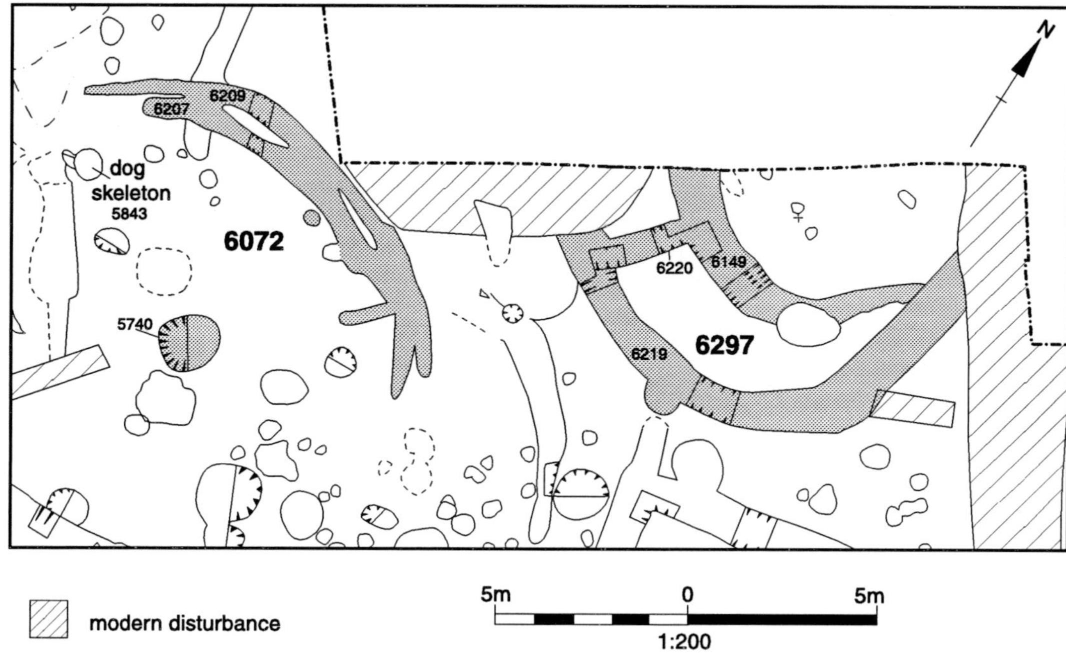

Figure 2.18 Structure 6297 and windbreak feature 6072

oriented broadly east-west with the points of the semicircle pointing towards the south. Where sectioned the two gullies were of very similar profile and character. The outer gully 6209 produced a small amount of middle Iron Age pottery whilst the inner gully 6207 contained a single sherd of early/middle Iron Age pottery. A linear feature which intersected the two curved gullies at their western end was not excavated and its relationship with them is unknown.

A number of pits and postholes were revealed immediately to the south of 6072. It is possible that the postholes once held a timber-framed structure of some kind but there was no discernible building plan. A small pit (5843) located *c* 2 m to the south-west of the 'windbreak' contained an articulated dog skeleton. Only one pit in the vicinity (5740) was positively dated to the middle Iron Age, and it is unclear if it was associated with 6072 or should be seen as part of a linear pitted zone which ran toward the east in this area (see below).

A second 'windbreak' type feature (6306) similar to 6072 in plan lay *c* 2 m to the north-east and a third (6307) *c* 9 m to the south-west (Fig. 2.13). Neither of these features were as well-preserved as 6072. Structure 6307 in particular was difficult to define and it is possible that its apparently similar form is misleading. All three features faced the same direction however, with the external curve of the semicircle facing the north.

Structure 6301 *(Fig. 2.13)*

Structure 6301 was located 5 m south-west of 6307. It was of broadly similar plan and could be a fourth example of the 'windbreak' type feature. Unlike the other examples however, it was a single ditched feature and was more substantial than the narrow gullies which made up the other features.

Boundary ditch 6298 (Fig. 2.19)

Feature 6298 comprised north-east - south-west ditch 6299 and a complex sequence of north-west - south-east ditches (6300) which together formed a T-shaped enclosure or boundary in the north-west corner of Trench 33. The ditch 6299 may have marked the north-west boundary of Iron Age domestic occupation and it may not be a coincidence that the later Roman ditch 5359 ran parallel to 6299 for a distance of 20 m.

Ditch 6299

Ditch 6299 was linear in plan and contained a relatively complex sequence of deposits. It was 1.4 m wide at the top and had a steep sided, V-shaped profile which tapered to a narrow (0.10 m) flat-bottomed slot at the base (Fig. 2.20). The slot was presumably designed to hold timber uprights.

Ditch complex 6300

Ditch complex 6300 consisted of a complicated sequence of ditches and gullies which together formed a north-west - south-east linear feature running at right-angles to, and apparently cut by, 6299. Insufficient investigation due to time limitations precluded a full understanding of this area but it would seem that 6300 originally terminated to the north-west of 6299 creating an entranceway some 5 m wide. Subsequent re-modelling of the area would seem to have blocked the entranceway with a series of ditches and gullies.

Well 5664 (Fig. 2.19)

Just over 25 % of this feature was excavated revealing near vertical edges which had partially collapsed in

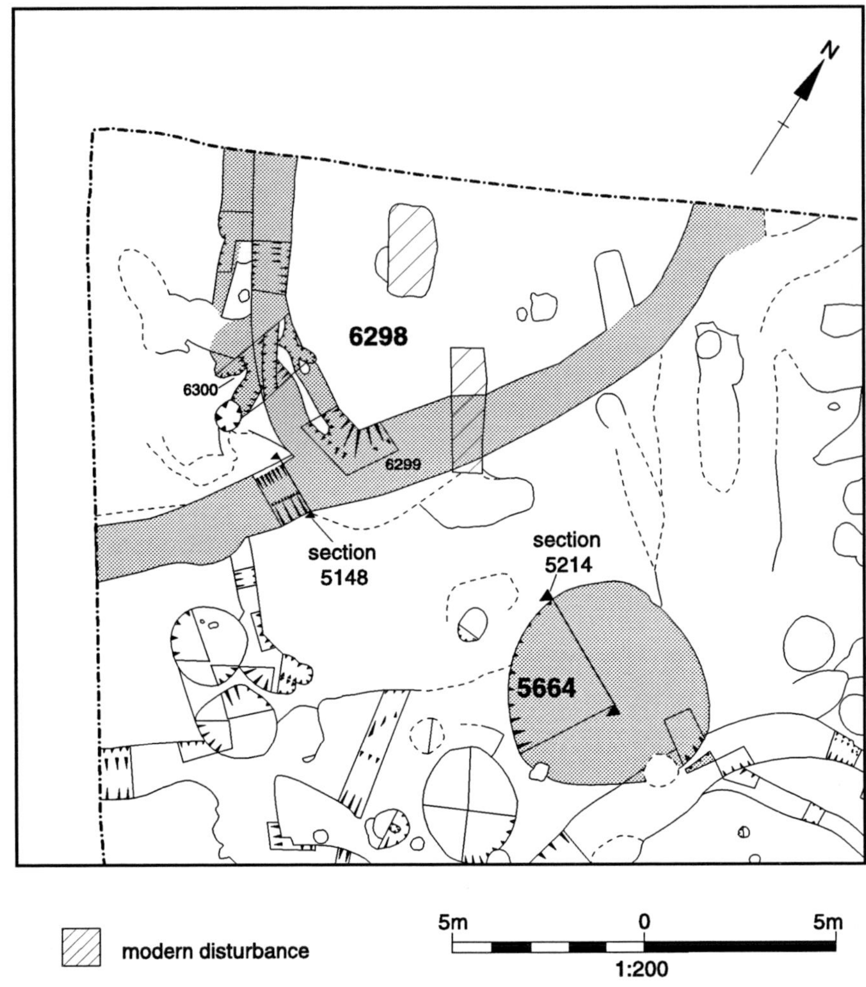

Figure 2.19 Boundary ditch 6298 and well 5664

places, and a flattish base (Fig. 2.21). The well was approximately circular measuring 5-5.5 m across x 1.6 m deep and was filled with numerous deposits which produced middle Iron Age pottery from the top to the very bottom of the feature. Soil samples were taken to assess the environmental potential of the feature and produced good results (Chapter 4).

The Roman period *(Fig. 2.22)*

Enclosure 5978

Structure 5978 was an open-ended square enclosure (*c* 10 m x 10 m). Its southern side was defined by the larger Roman ditch 5359. The structure appeared to have no eastern side but this may have been obscured by modern disturbance. The enclosure ditch had steep, straight edges with a flat bottom and was 1.10 m in width x *c* 0.45 m deep. A linear ditch oriented north-west by south-east appeared to divide the interior of the enclosure. This feature, however, was cut by the enclosure ditch (5978) and was therefore not contemporary.

Ditch 5359

Linear ditch 5359 crossed the whole of Trench 33. The feature ran from the south-east corner to the centre of the site (*c* 40 m in length) where it was lost among unexcavated soil marks. A ditch of similar profile (V-shaped with straight sides) and containing contemporary pottery ran towards the east from this point and was probably the return of 5359 (40 m in length). Both lengths of ditch appeared to narrow as they approached the centre of the site and it is possible that a small entrance existed at that point. Although the ditch did not respect the Iron Age roundhouse structures, it did run broadly parallel to the Iron Age boundary ditch 6299 suggesting that to some extent the earlier form of the settlement was still reflected by local conditions.

Pits (Fig 2.23)

Method and classification

A total of 51 pits out of an estimated 77 (66.2 %) were excavated in Trench 33. The majority were half-sectioned in order to determine the feature profile and to recover dating evidence. Basic data concerning dimension, shape, and profile was recovered from all excavated pits in an attempt to produce a crude classification of pit types. Of the data types, pit profile seemed to be the most promising data set and was used as the basis for classification. Pit type A consisted of flat-based cylindrical pits with steep or vertical sides. Type B consisted of bowl-shaped pits with moderately steep sides, and Type C consisted of shallow saucer-like pits.

It was hoped that such a classification might be used to determine pit function and through that to illuminate certain aspects of the site economy. Many of the pits were heavily truncated by later features, however, and the majority could not be clearly placed within any given pit type. The resulting reduced data set was so small (23 pits) that analysis proved to be largely inconclusive.

Environmental evidence

Although classification through profile alone proved to be disappointing, a few pits did contain environmental evidence of interest. A total of five pits contained cereal grain or chaff within their fills. Four of those pits were type A, suggesting that the flat-based cylindrical pits may have been used for grain storage. Pit 5740 in particular contained relatively high quantities of wheat grain and spelt (Fig. 2.18).

Chronology

Over two thirds of the excavated pits (72.5%) were initially assigned to broad chronological groups based upon pottery types. By far the largest number of excavated pits was assigned to the middle Iron Age with smaller but significant numbers dating to the early / middle Iron Age. Only two pits were dated to the late Iron Age (Table 2.1).

Postholes

A total of 140 postholes were excavated out of an estimated 421 in Trench 33. Of the excavated postholes 51 contained pottery and pottery was collected from the surface of another 18 (Table 2.2). The pottery dates ranged from the early to middle Iron Age. By comparing Table 2.1 and Table 2.2 it becomes clear that the postholes contained a far higher percentage of early/middle Iron Age pottery than the pits. This would seem to suggest that posthole structures or postholes were more common in the early to middle Iron Age than in later periods.

There were six main clusters of postholes in Trench 33, two of which were particularly dense (Fig. 2.24). Although it was relatively easy to draw out post-built structures from the clusters, deciding which were genuine was more difficult. The nature of the problem is well illustrated by the fact that in some cases the same posthole could be used equally well for more than one structure.

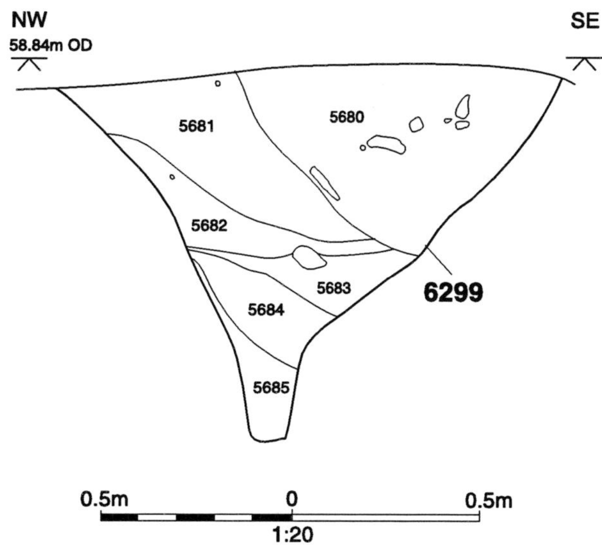

Figure 2.20 Section through boundary ditch 6299

Posthole alignment 6312 (Fig. 2.24)

Posthole alignment 6312 may have marked a fenceline. The alignment was oriented north-south with an east-west arm forming a T-shaped junction. Not all of the postholes were excavated but those that were proved to be quite substantial (*c* 0.40 m wide x 0.45–0.60 m deep) with a hint of a postpipe in some cases. Phasing the structure is difficult as no stratigraphic relationships existed with other features and the pottery recovered was too small to be identified. The alignment of the

Table 2.1 Excavated pits (by phase)

	No.	%
E/MIA	9	19.6
MIA	25	49.0
LIA	2	3.9
Undated	14	27.5

Table 2.2 Postholes containing pottery (by phase)

	No.	%
E/MIA	42	60.9
MIA	27	39.1
All periods	69	

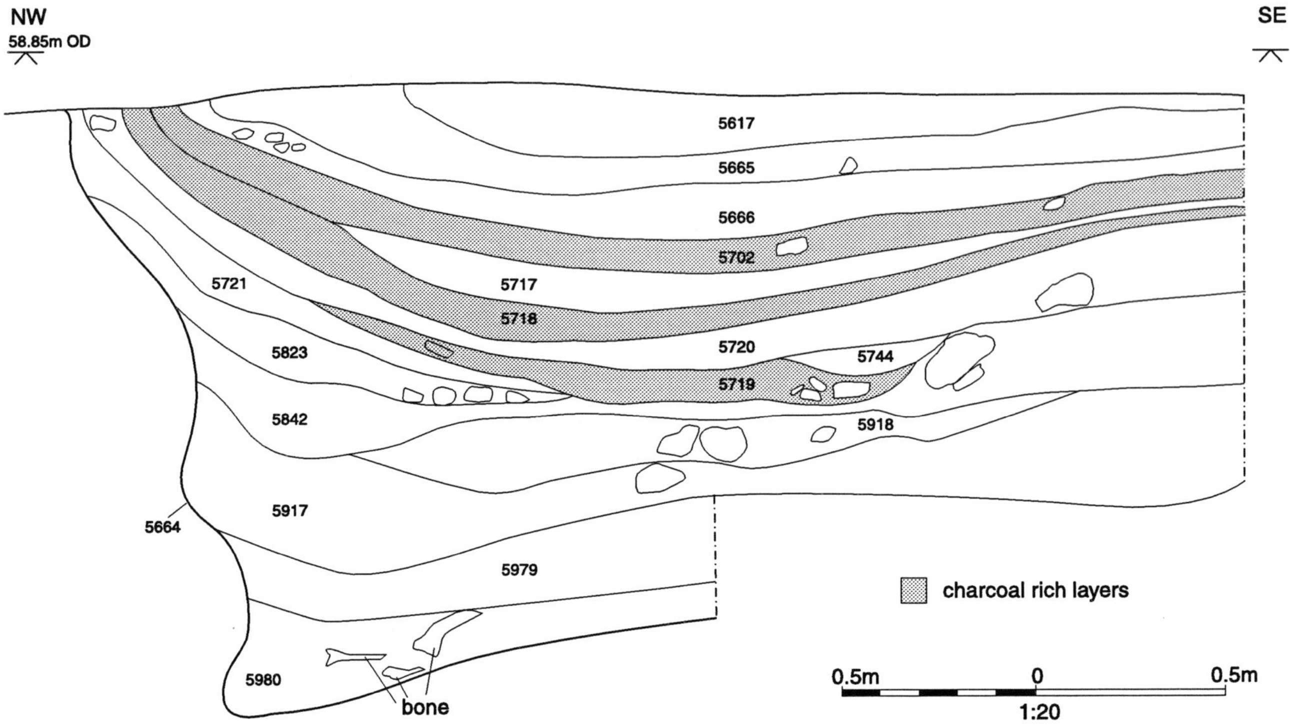

Figure 2.21 Section through well 5664

structure was such that it did not obviously relate to other features in the vicinity. It is possible that the structure predates the Iron Age, but there was no clue as to what its function may have been.

***Posthole cluster 6313** (Fig. 2.24)*

Posthole cluster 6313 was located beneath the western half of structure 5021. Although clearly a discreet posthole group, 6313 did not form an obvious structure and has already been described above.

***Posthole clusters 6314 and 6315** (Fig. 2.24)*

Two dense clusters of postholes were revealed towards the centre of the site. It was thought during the excavation that the postholes may have formed twin rectangular structures. Analysis in post-excavation, however, isolated four examples of possible round-houses (5087, 5257, 5166 and 6310) and it seems probable that the rectangular structures were illusory (Fig.2.10).

***Posthole cluster 6316** (Fig. 2.24)*

A small group of insubstantial postholes were identified within structure 6283. Early Iron Age pottery was recovered from three of the postholes (Fig. 2.15). It is uncertain if the postholes were associated with 6283 or formed part of an earlier timber-built structure.

***Posthole cluster 6317** (Fig. 2.24)*

Posthole cluster 6317 was located in the eastern corner of the site adjacent to structure 6286. No obvious structures were identified within it.

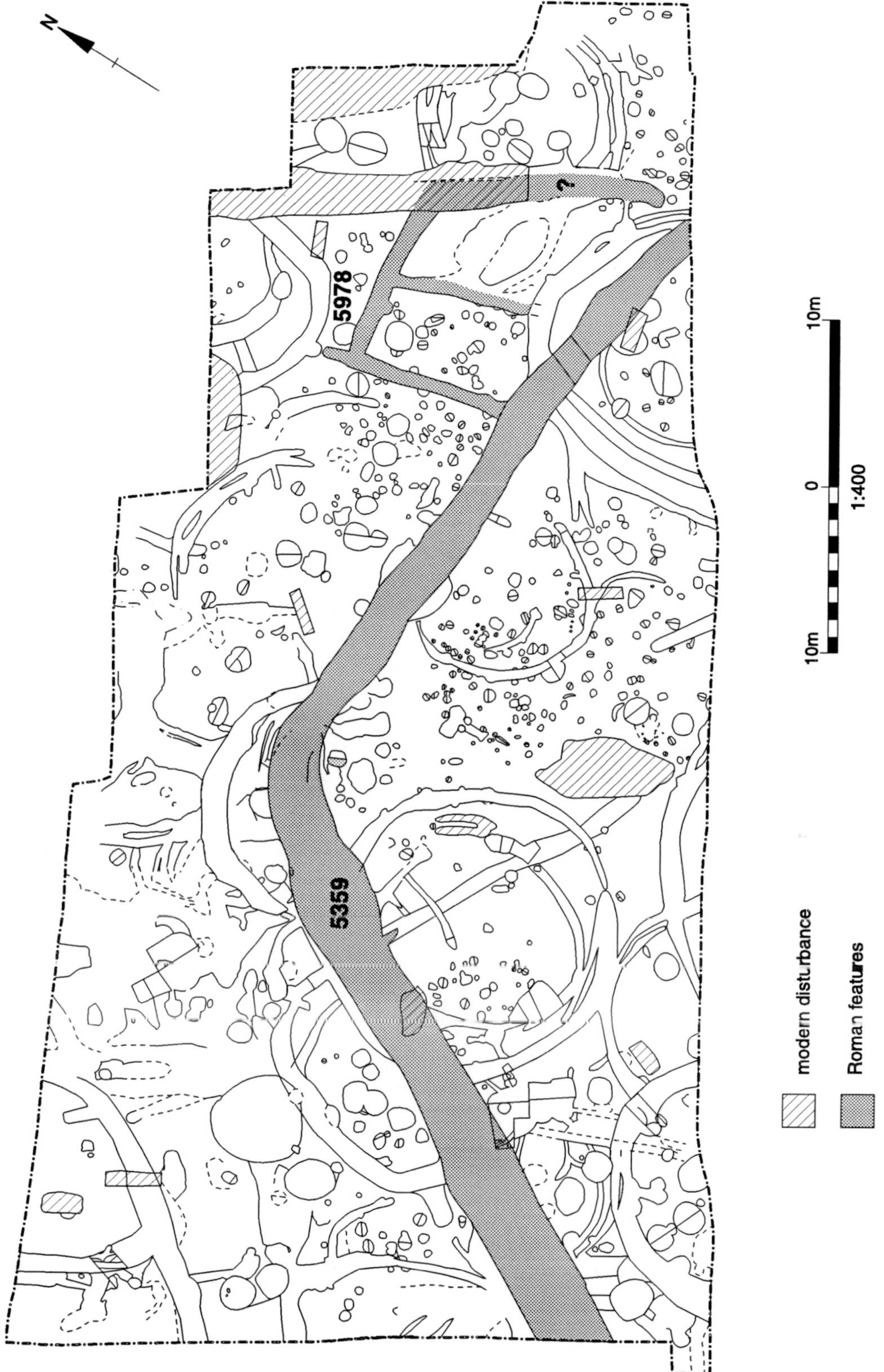

Figure 2.22 The Roman period (Trench 33)

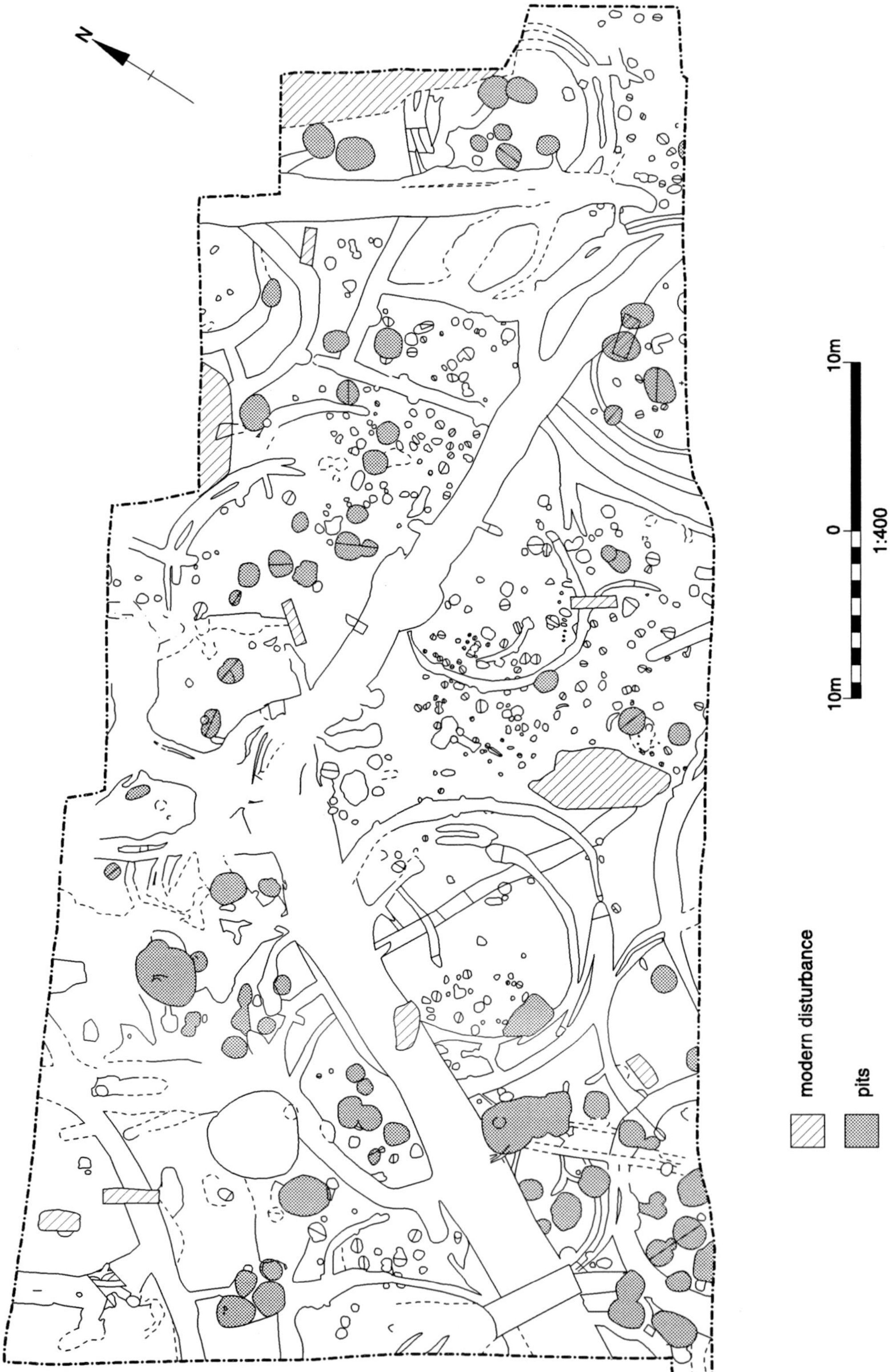

Figure 2.23 Pit distribution, all periods (Trench 33)

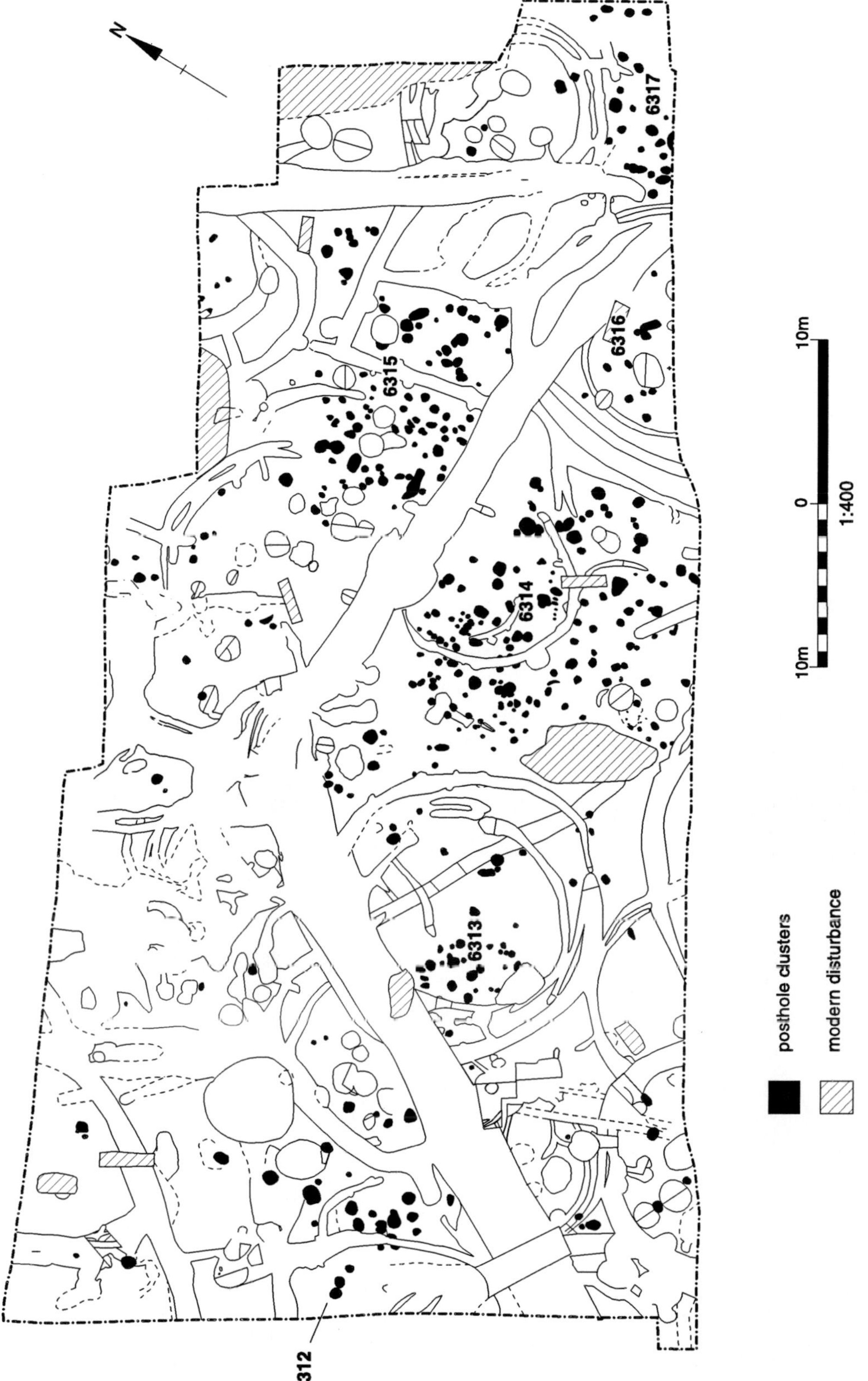

Figure 2.24 Posthole distribution, all periods (Trench 33)

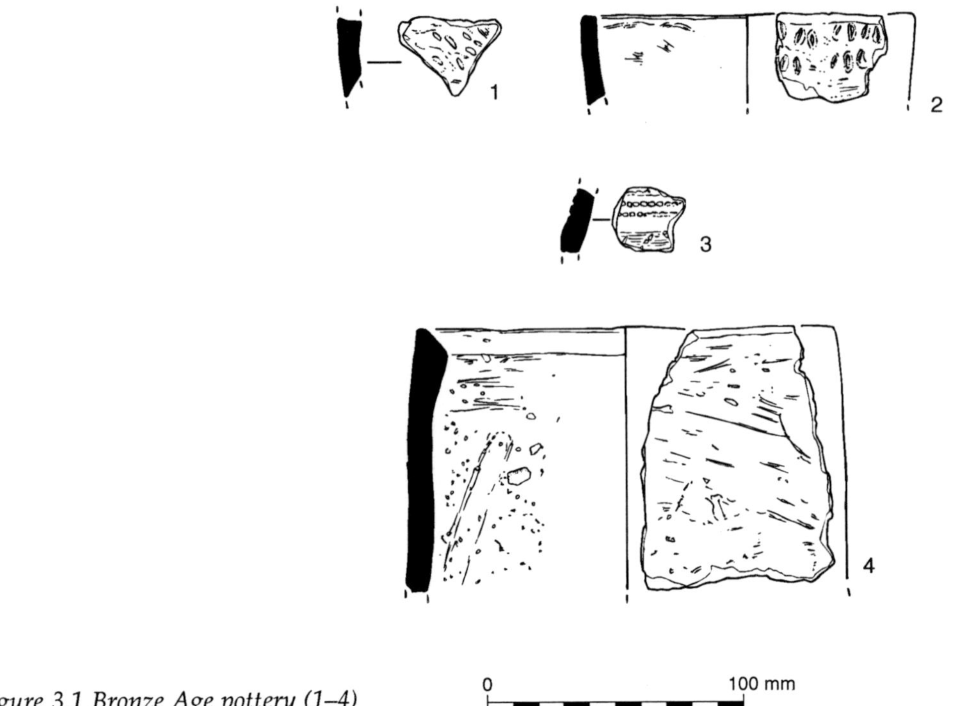

Figure 3.1 Bronze Age pottery (1–4)

Table 3.1 Structures and features with 20 or more sherds from early and middle Iron Age periods

	Fabric group											
Structure (S)/ feature (F)	A calcareous	B sand	C sand/lime	D iron	E iron/lime	F flint	G grog	H grog/lime	I organic	U unclassif	later intrusive	Total
EIA												
S6286	70	24	2	0	0	0	0	1	0	0	0	97
S6287	14	6	0	0	0	0	0	0	0	0	0	20
Pit 5221	20	4	3	1	0	0	0	0	0	17	0	45
Pit 5522	6	6	7	1	0	0	0	0	0	0	0	20
Pit 5960	43	3	2	0	0	0	0	1	0	15	1	64
MIA												
S5021	90	49	29	6	13	2	2	0	1	20	0	212
S6282	21	12	15	23	2	0	0	0	0	16	0	89
S6290	32	25	3	0	1	0	0	0	0	0	0	61
S6291	15	7	3	0	0	0	0	0	0	0	0	25
S6297	18	10	0	2	0	0	4	0	0	0	0	34
S6298	419	144	13	27	62	2	3	0	0	47	0	717
Well 5664	141	81	0	10	2	1	0	0	0	4	1	240
F5361	76	1	0	2	0	0	0	0	0	0	0	90
Pit 5153	5	21	2	0	0	0	0	0	0	7	0	35
Pit 5179	6	4	3	0	4	0	0	0	1	4	0	22
Pit 5270	3	0	0	0	49	0	0	0	0	18	0	70
Pit 5361	45	14	1	15	4	0	0	0	0	28	0	107
Pit 5369	29	4	0	1	0	0	0	0	0	0	0	34
Pit 5372	24	17	0	1	0	0	0	0	0	21	0	63
Pit 5504	12	3	0	1	1	0	0	0	0	17	0	34
Pit 5540	15	8	6	0	0	0	1	0	0	1	0	31
Pit 5569	289	11	3	0	2	0	1	0	0	0	0	306
Pit 5641	10	8	3	0	0	0	0	0	0	0	0	21
Pit 5740	14	9	1	1	0	0	0	0	0	5	0	30
Pit 6238	19	15	2	0	0	0	0	0	0	0	0	36
Gully 5819	15	6	0	0	0	0	0	0	0	0	0	21
Gully 5919	4	68	1	0	0	0	0	0	0	0	0	73

Chapter 3: The Finds

THE POTTERY *by Jane Timby*

Introduction

The pottery assemblage comprises some 5290 sherds, weighing 66.285 kg. Whilst the bulk of the wares appear to date to the early and middle Iron Age periods, sherds of earlier and later Bronze Age, and Roman date are present, along with twelve medieval and three post-medieval pieces. Approximately 90% of the pottery was recovered from the main 1994 excavation (trenches 29, 32 and 33), the remainder coming from the preceding evaluation work. Trench 33 produced by far the greatest amount of material, some 4843 sherds compared to 82 from Trench 32, and 263 from Trench 29. The assemblage was of variable condition with some very friable pieces resulting in a high breakage rate, but also several larger sherds, often from the same vessels. The assemblage has a relatively good average sherd size of 12.5 g. The surface condition of most of the sherds is good.

The Wyndyke Furlong assemblage is a useful addition to the larger collection of wares published by De Roche (1978) from the Ashville trading estate, Abingdon, which forms part of the same settlement complex. Whilst many of the wares are paralleled in the published material there is much new detailed information - in particular, additional forms and more refined fabric groups - from the Wyndyke Furlong group to complement the older assemblage. Information about the Ashville assemblage is based on the published report; the pottery was not looked at by the author.

The pottery from Wyndyke Furlong was recovered from 427 individual contexts. In many cases several contexts belonged to one feature. Of the 427 contexts only 5% contained more than 50 sherds, 9% between 20 and 49 sherds, and 86% produced less than 20 sherds. Approximately 50% of this latter group had less than five sherds. This, combined with a significant lack of chronologically diagnostic forms and fabrics, and in some contexts an apparent high level of redeposition, has severely limited the extent to which it is possible to reliably date some features on ceramic grounds.

Methodology

The sherds were sorted into fabric types on the basis of the main inclusions present. Further subtypes were distinguished on the basis of the grade and relative proportions of inclusions visible. The complexity of the fabric range meant that most sherds needed to be examined using a binocular microscope (x20). Unfortunately this was not a practical option given the time constraints for the work. As a result some less distinctive wares may have not have been distinguished. This may be true in particular for those wares containing finer fragments of recent (ie alluvial) versus fossil shell. Very small sherds and material recovered from sieving were not sorted into fabrics but simply counted and weighed. The sorted fabrics were recorded by weight, sherd count and estimated vessel equivalents (EVEs) for each context. The data was entered into a computer spreadsheet (Excel) which forms part of the archive.

In the following report the pottery is discussed chronologically using the information from each of the three main trenches. A detailed description of the fabrics can be found in Appendix A. A selection of the better preserved sherds has been illustrated.

Discussion

Earlier prehistoric pottery

Most of the earlier prehistoric pottery was concentrated in Trench 33 - including a small group of diagnostically Bronze Age sherds - but occurred largely as redeposited finds in later contexts. The only possible exceptions are F5279 (5278) and posthole 5226 where Beaker sherds were the only pottery present. The latter feature may be associated with roundhouse structure 5257 (see below).

The earlier prehistoric material from Trench 33 includes five sherds of Beaker (from contexts 5569, 5475, 5582, 5278 and 5226) and one from an urn (5664). Of the Beaker sherds, two - a rim (5278) and a bodysherd (5226) - are decorated with fingernail impressions, the latter set randomly (Fig. 3.1, 1–2). Similar Beakers with fingernail decoration have been found at Cassington (Case *et al.* 1964–5, fig. 22, 1–6). Of the remaining sherds two are plain and one (5569) has cord-impressed decoration (Fig. 3.1, 3). Four of the sherds are characterised by a moderately fine, grog-tempered fabric; the piece from 5226 contained grog but displayed a slightly sandy texture with sparse flint and iron. A single sherd of cord-impressed Beaker also came from Trench 29 (75). This sherd contained fine, rounded, ill-sorted quartz sand with fine grog.

A rimsherd from F5664 (5918) has characteristics which suggest it might belong to the Deverel-Rimbury tradition. The rim is internally bevelled and belongs to an urn-like vessel with plain vertical walls, 8–9 mm thick (Fig. 3.1, 4). The vessel is dark grey-brown in colour, paler brown on the interior. The paste contains sparse fossil shell up to 4–5 mm in size and rounded red-brown iron. Internally bevelled rims from biconical urns were recovered from cremations associated with a ring ditch on the eastern side of Abingdon (Balkwill 1978, 25–8, fig. 27). A middle Bronze Age date was ascribed to these vessels on the basis of associated ring-headed pins and comparison with other material from the Thames Valley. A similar internally bevelled rim was present amongst Bronze Age pottery published from Long Wittenham (Case *et al.* 1964–5, fig. 29, 3).

Posthole F5024 (5023) produced eleven sherds (976 g) from the base of a large thick-walled (10–12 mm) plain urn-like vessel in a very coarse fossil shell fabric.

The flat base has a diameter of 260 mm. Accompanying the coarse sherds is a thin-walled, black, finer shell-tempered slack-sided jar with a smooth finish and an orange, sandy ware with grog tempering possibly from a Beaker.

Contexts 5040 and 5962 in ditch S6304, Trench 33, also placed into the earlier prehistoric sequence, contained five bodysherds (fabrics L1, SL and unclassified fragments). None of the pieces is particularly diagnostic and the fabrics also occur in Iron Age contexts.

It is highly likely that other redeposited sherds may also be of Bronze Age date, but in the absence of featured pieces, and with the fragmentary state of many of the sherds, it is difficult to be certain.

Iron Age pottery

The Iron Age assemblage is dominated by coarseware fabrics augmented by a small number of fine wares. The latter includes, for the early Iron Age, sherds of thinner-walled, sharply carinated bowls and at least eight sherds of haematite-coated ware (Fabric S9).

In total some 36 fabrics have been defined for the Iron Age material which can be condensed into nine broad ware groups:

- A - calcareous (limestone only or limestone and shell-tempered)
- B - sandy wares
- C - sand and limestone
- D - ferruginous wares (with distinct grains of iron)
- E - iron and limestone-tempered
- F - flint-tempered
- G - grog-tempered
- H - grog and limestone-tempered
- I - organic.

A quantified summary of the individual fabrics can be found in Table 3.1. This includes only phased contexts.

Looking at the Iron Age assemblage as a whole (Table 3.2) the calcareous wares (limestone and/or shell-tempered wares) dominate, accounting for 52% by weight, followed by sandy wares at 28%. The remaining 20% is divided between the seven other defined ware groups and unclassified sherds, none of which exceeds 7%. The grog category includes several sherds of Bronze Age date.

Early Iron Age pottery

Approximately 6% by count of the assemblage comprises wares attributable to contexts stratigraphically placed in the early Iron Age (excluding redeposited material). The initial impression is that this group is dominated by coarse shell-tempered (L1) and limestone-tempered (L2, L3, SL) fabrics with smaller amounts of finer sandy fabrics (eg S9). Forms include a large bi-partite jar with fingertip decoration (Fig. 3.2, 5); expanded T-shaped or flanged rim jars (Fig. 3.2, 6, 15, 17, 19), slack-sided jars (Fig. 3.27) and carinated tripartite bowls (Fig. 3.2, 8). Finewares include haematite-slipped wares (fabric S9).

Table 3.2 Total quantities of later prehistoric pottery

Ware	Group	Weight (g)	%	No.	%	Eve	%
A	Calcareous	28223	52	1866	42	684	44
B	Sandy	15425	28	1330	30	523	34
C	Sand and limestone	3614	6.5	175	4	113	7
D	Iron	3441	6	201	4.5	134	8.5
E	Iron and limestone	2038	3.5	142	3	61	4
F	Flint	505	*	27	*	34	2
G	Grog	279	*	50	1	8	*
H	Grog and limestone	39	*	3	*	0	0
I	Organic	244	*	98	2	0	0
U	Unclassified	674	1	559	12.5	3	*
	Total	54482	100	4451	100	1560	100

Decoration includes finger depressions (Fig. 3.2, 9, 13–14 and Fig. 3.3, 32), impressed motifs such as the circles (Fig. 3.2, 21) and panel-type decoration with round depressions set within defined boundaries (Fig. 3.2, 18).

Much of the early Iron Age pottery came from the dense concentration of features found in Trench 33. Many of the postholes relating to the defined circular structures were ceramically poor. Table 3.3 lists the main wares from structures, pits and other features yielding in excess of 20 sherds. For the early Iron Age phase this is limited to S6286, S6287 and pits F5221, 5522 and 5960.

Six of the postholes relating to the structures S5257 and S5087 yielded a few sherds. Diagnostic pieces include a bodysherd from a sharply carinated vessel from F5088 (fabric L3) and a jar rim (fabric SL). Other fabrics present include L1, L2, S6 and SLa. Further early Iron Age sherds (fabrics L1, L2 and S1) were recovered from post-built structure S5166 including a haematite-slipped example from F5194. Structure S6310 was similarly ceramically poor with just seven sherds, mainly shelly wares. Structure S6287, which produced a total of 20 sherds amongst which was part of a slack-sided jar (Fig. 3.2, 7), typical of the early-middle Iron Age. Ring gully S6286 produced a relatively good group totalling 97 sherds including two haematite-slipped pieces along with fabrics S1–3, S6, L1–3, L6, SI, H1, I2 and SL. Sandy wares were particularly well represented compared to the other early Iron Age groups, perhaps indicating a date towards the early-middle Iron Age as regionally there appears to be an increase in sandy wares in the middle Iron Age. Pit 5221 contained 46 sherds with a mixture of limestone and sand-tempered wares. Further early Iron Age material came from posthole F5024 alongside sherds of a Bronze Age urn. Other groups of 20 or more sherds came from pit F5522 including a carinated bowl (S4), and pit F5960 (Fig. 3.2,14–17) with a number of fingertip decorated sherds and internally flanged vessels.

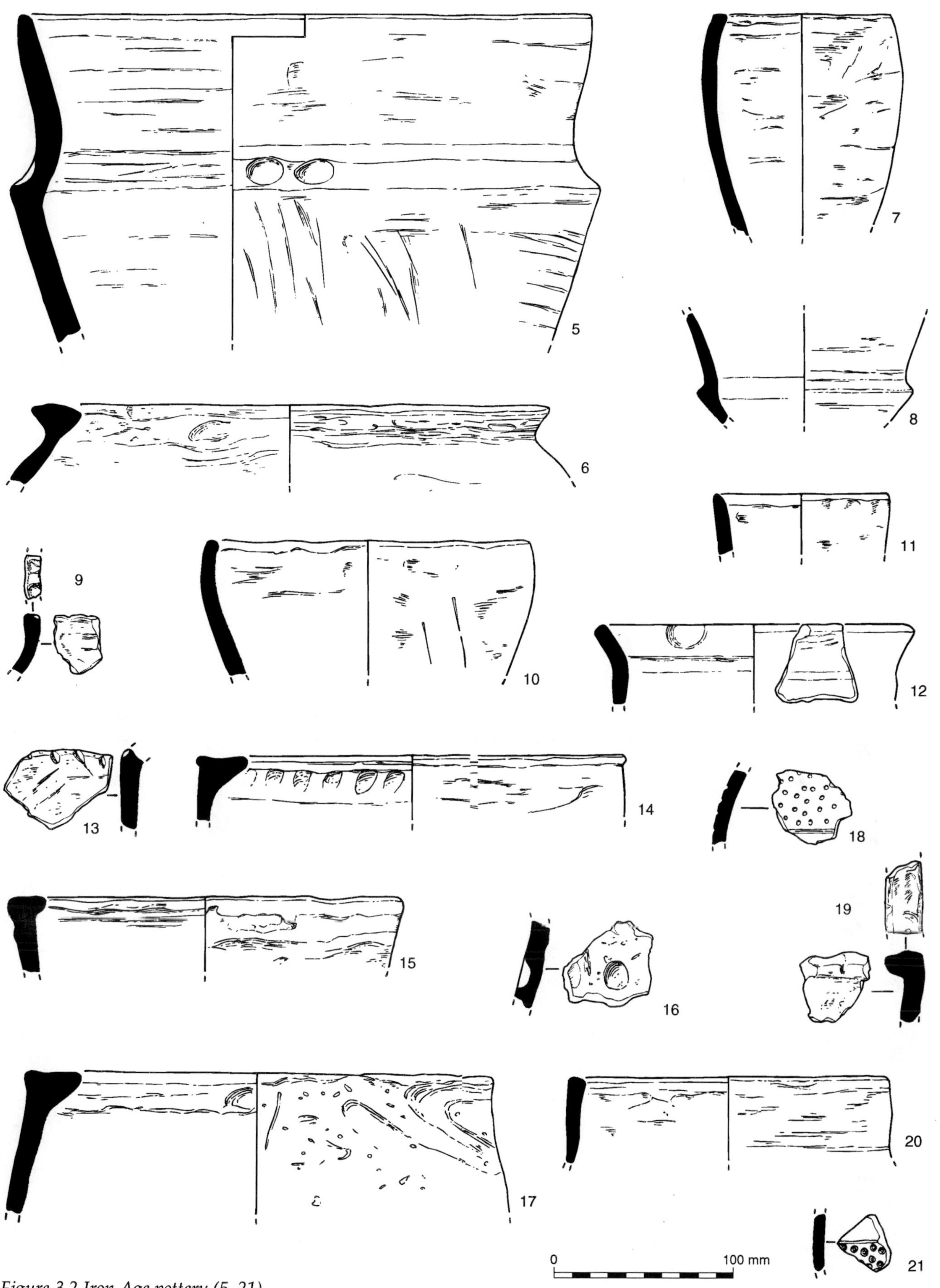

Figure 3.2 Iron Age pottery (5–21)

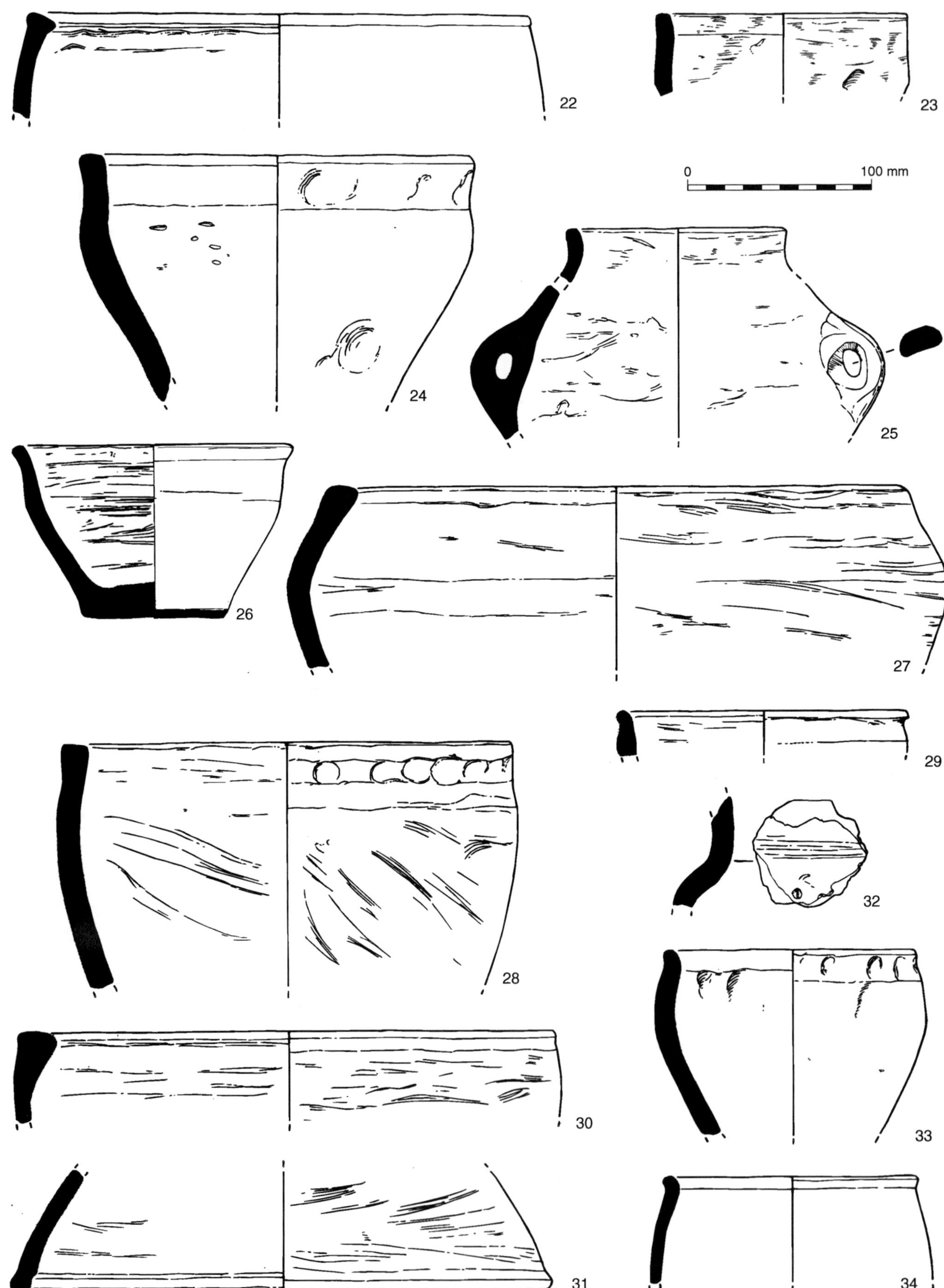

Figure 3.3 Iron Age pottery (22–34)

Table 3.3 Quantities of Iron Age fabrics from phased contexts (excluding redeposited or unphased material)

Group	Fabric	EIA/ MIA		MIA		MIA/ LIA	
		No.	Weight (g)	No.	Weight (g)	No.	Weight (g)
A	L1	138	2277	425	7561	24	260
	L2	22	290	161	2463	3	26
	L3	35	933	259	3665	10	81
	L4	5	45	148	1895	0	0
	L5	0	0	1	19	0	0
	L6	9	102	25	276	0	0
	L7	0	0	40	826	0	0
	L00	5	59	26	786	2	73
B	S1	11	62	221	3105	29	173
	S2	3	39	139	1753	15	134
	S3	2	6	82	664	2	52
	S4	8	117	76	882	17	112
	S5	0	0	35	484	6	122
	S6	6	119	114	1544	9	96
	S7	5	150	7	136	3	15
	S8	1	27	29	195	2	18
	S9	2	16	4	14	1	5
	S00	5	27	20	213	2	19
C	SL	25	1340	114	1686	5	75
D	I1	2	30	31	356	14	42
	I2	2	11	59	708	0	0
	SI	1	15	3	28	0	0
E	IL1	0	0	63	654	0	0
	IL2	0	0	62	1102	3	25
	ISL	0	0	1	2	0	0
F	F1	0	0	1	9	0	0
	FS	0	0	1	2	0	0
	FI	0	0	3	131	0	0
G	G2	0	0	35	139	0	0
	G4	0	0	4	23	0	0
	GS1	0	0	0	0	4	116
	GS2	0	0	0	0	1	12
	GS	1	9	4	67	0	0
	GF	0	0	2	105	0	0
	GL	1	30	2	9	0	0
I	O1	0	0	6	30	0	0
U	unclass	33	48	294	454	31	24
Early Prehist.		11	976	6	32	0	0
Roman		3	12	1	24	0	0
Med.		0	0	1	10	0	0
Total		336	6740	2505	32052	183	1480

Middle Iron Age pottery

By analogy with material found elsewhere in the Thames Valley, the bulk of the assemblage from Wyndyke Furlong, in excess of 2500 sherds, broadly dates to the middle Iron Age period (*c* 4th–2nd centuries BC). Although calcareous wares still dominate, following trends noted elsewhere in the Thames Valley (Lambrick 1984; Allen 1990a, 34), the proportion of sandy wares and sandy and limestone-tempered wares increases. A number of new fabrics appear in the ceramic record for the first time (cf Table 3.3). Of particular note are iron-tempered wares, in particular one with distinctive oolitic grains (fabric I2) and a limestone and iron-tempered ware (IL1–2, ISL). Also present are small numbers of flint-tempered, organic-tempered and grog-tempered sherds.

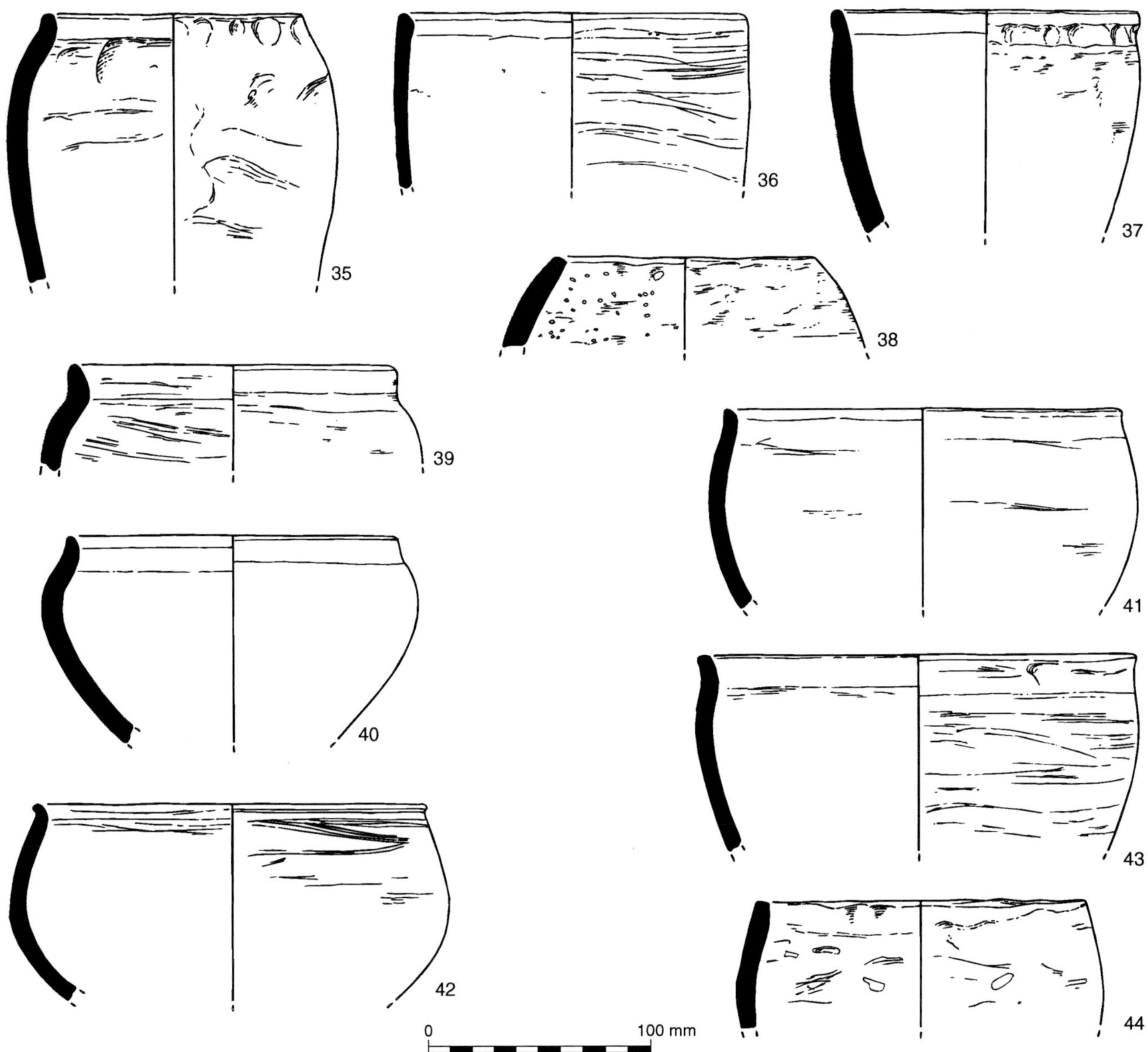

Figure 3.4 Iron Age pottery (35–44)

The range of forms largely replicates that found on other Middle Iron Age sites in the Thames Valley, adding little to the repertoire already published from the site (cf De Roche 1978). Similar wares have been published recently, for example, from Watkins Farm, Northmoor (Allen 1990a), Farmoor (Lambrick 1979), Mingies Ditch (D Wilson 1993) and Whitehouse Road, Oxford (Mudd 1993), and largely comprise plain, coarse jars and bowls. The diameters of the various jars/bowls range from 100 mm to 340 mm with a peak around 160–80 mm. Included in the Wyndyke Furlong repertoire are barrel-bodied jars (Figs 3.3, 34; 3.4, 35, 38), one with countersunk handles (Fig. 3.3, 25), vertical-walled jars reminiscent of Wessex-style saucepan pots with slightly thickened rims (Fig. 3.4, 36); slack-sided jars with squared (Fig. 3.3, 28) or slightly beaded rims (Figs 3.2, 10; 3.4, 37) and round-based and globular bodied jars (Figs 3.3, 33; 3.4, 38). Bowls included small hand-sized examples (Fig. 3.3, 23), wide-mouthed types (Fig. 3.3, 24, 26) and globular-bodied examples with small shaped rims (Fig. 3.4, 39–44). There are a few particularly large bowl-like vessels with slightly thickened rims (Fig. 3.3, 22, 27, 30). A single domed lid (Fig. 3.3, 31) was present in the middle Iron Age contexts.

Most of the vessels had a roughly smoothed, matt finish. Burnishing was mainly limited to the globular bowls and decorated pieces were rare. Sandy wares tended to show a higher incidence of burnishing compared to the calcareous class. In the assemblage as a whole only two sherds showed any formal type of decoration other than finger-impressed (Fig. 3.2, 18, 21). A sherd (fabric L2) from 5590 had an irregular scored surface.

Table 3.4 Total quantities of later Iron Age / Roman wares

Type	Fabrics	Description	Weight (g)	%	No.	%	Eve	%
Import	SAM	Samian	92	*	9	1	2	*
Regional	SAVGT	Savernake	558	5	17	2	6	*
	DORBB1	Dorset black burnished ware	14	*	1	*	0	0
	WILOX	N Wilts oxidised	4	*	2	*	0	0
	WILRE	N Wilts reduced	174	1.5	17	2	48	5
Local	OXFRE	Oxon reduced ware	1383	12	131	15	250	28
	OXFOX	Oxon oxidised ware	1115	9.5	70	8	65	7
	OXFWS	Oxon white-slipped ware	30	*	1	*	0	0
	OXFWH1	Oxon sandy whiteware	104	*	8	1	0	0
	OXFWH2	Oxon fine whiteware	170	1.5	15	2	0	0
	OXFWHM	Oxon whiteware mortaria	61	*	4	*	10	*
	OXFRC	Oxon colour-coated ware	3	*	1	*	0	0
	OXID	Miscellaneous oxidised sandy	46	*	14	1.5	0	0
	GREY	Miscellaneous grey /black sandy	228	2	25	3	25	3
	GREY1	Local grey ware	3	*	1	*	0	0
	GREY2	Local grey ware	746	6.5	78	9	99	11
	GREY3	Local grey ware	229	2	17	2	26	3
	GREY4	Local grey ware	667	6	50	6	73	8
	GREY5	Local grey ware	1714	14.5	109	13	102	11
	GREY6	Local grey ware	39	*	4	*	0	0
	GREY7	Local grey ware	40	*	7	*	2	*
	GREY8	Local grey ware	813	7	46	5	1	*
	GREY9	Local grey ware	300	2.5	9	1	17	*
	GREY10	Local grey ware	119	1	9	1	28	3
	GREY11	Local grey ware	168	1.5	4	*	26	3
	WW	Miscellaneous whiteware	89	*	4	*	0	0
	GROG	Grog-tempered	2468	21	172	20	87	10
	GROG/LIME	Grog and limestone	268	2	29	3	34	4
	GROG/FLINT	Grog and flint	40	*	1	*	0	0
Totals			11685	100	855	100	901	100

* = less than 1%

Several vessels showed some evidence of use, mainly in the form of exterior or interior sooting. Some of the calcareous group vessels showed internal surface leaching. Sherds from 5633 (fabric L1), 6185 (fabric L7) and 5002 (fabric S1) had internal calcareous concretions from holding water.

Later Iron Age – Roman pottery

Sherds of later Iron Age-Roman date accounted for 14% by count and weight of the total recovered assemblage and 32% by EVEs, the latter reflecting to a certain extent the better survival rate of this material. This figure includes the various grog-tempered wares considered still to be in use throughout the 1st century AD. With the exception of one or two odd sherds most of the Roman assemblage proper appears to belong to the 1st–2nd centuries. Table 3.4 summarises the main fabrics identified. Grog-tempered wares account for between 20–24% by sherd number and may suggest occupation of the site from the earlier part of the 1st century AD. The assemblage mainly comprises wares from local industries and, with the exception of just nine sherds of samian, there are no continental imports. Regional imports also appear to be limited, being restricted to sherds of Savernake ware, a single sherd of Dorset black-burnished ware and some possible North Wiltshire products. Over half the group comprises grey or black wares presumed to derive from local sources.

The majority of the Roman wares were recovered from Trench 33. A particularly large group of material, comprising some 1045 sherds (15,645g), 81% of the entire assemblage from this period, was recovered from the linear feature S5359, and a smaller group of some 12 sherds from the square enclosure S5978.

The latest material associated with S5359 includes an Oxfordshire whiteware mortarium, various grey-wares and a Dorset black-burnished straight-sided dish suggesting a date of final abandonment in the mid-later 2nd century, unless it was intrusive or from surface layers. The feature also contained a range of grey and black sandy wares including jars, beakers (Fig. 3.5, 45) and a few oxidised wares including a barbotine decorated bowl (Fig. 3.5, 46) dating to the later 1st-early 2nd century (Young 1977, type O42). Redeposited Iron Age material accounts for 29% by sherd count (32% by weight) of the group, emphasising the disturbed nature

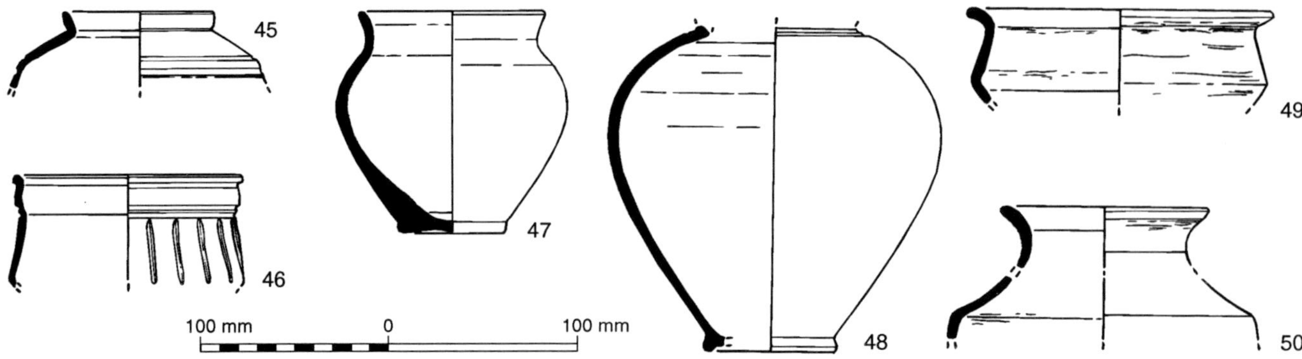

Figure 3.5 Roman pottery (45–50)

of the site. Apart from local fine grey and oxidised sandy wares there were no imported finewares in this group of material. Vessels of especial note include a small jar (Fig. 3.5, 47), an oxidised sandy ware jar with a broken rim ground down for re-use (Fig. 3.5, 48) and a carinated bowl (Fig. 3.5, 49) and jar (Fig. 3.5, 50).

The small group of wares from S5978 comprise seven Iron Age sandy wares, three sherds of Savernake ware and two Roman greywares. A broad date at the end of the 1st century or early 2nd century may be appropriate for the abandonment of this enclosure.

The range of wares from Wyndyke Furlong is thus much less diverse than that from the Ashville site which spans the 1st-4th centuries and in particular show a strong late Roman presence (Miles 1978a) not witnessed here. This would seem to imply a shifting settlement focus within the Roman period in the immediate area.

Summary

The assemblage from Wyndyke Furlong closely mirrors that from the adjacent Ashville Trading Estate (De Roche 1978). Most of the technological and typological trends noted for the Ashville material apply to the Wyndyke Furlong assemblage and are thus not reiterated in detail here. Although most of the wares could potentially be locally produced, the oolitic iron-tempered wares not previously identified, and perhaps the glauconitic sandy wares, suggest wider regional links (see Chapter 5). A detailed research programme field-testing local geologically available materials against the petrology of the pottery fabrics may provide a valuable insight into the extent and intensity of such trade versus local production. The initial impression is that an increasing diversity of fabrics in the Middle Iron Age indicates a more diverse economy and increased regional contact.

The small amount of early-middle Bronze pottery indicates a low level of earlier prehistoric activity in the area, traces of which were largely obliterated by subsequent Iron Age and Roman use of the site. Occupation starts in earnest in the early Iron Age and continues into the Middle Iron Age. There may well be a short hiatus in the ceramic record in the later Iron Age with a new phase of use starting in the 1st century AD. The apparent absence of a clear-cut late Iron Age phase, however, is a phenomenon noted elsewhere in the Abingdon area where Middle Iron Age forms and decorative schemes appear to continue into the 1st century AD (Allen 1997b). Subsequent work on assemblages in the immediate locality suggests that Period 3 at Ashville, dated to the Late Iron Age (Belgic) period, should in fact be a little later. Recent work on the finewares in the area suggests a local Abingdon production in the early Roman (Claudio-Neronian) period producing butt beakers and allied forms (Timby *et al.* 1997). This would push the abandonment of some of the Ashville features, in particular ditch 392 (De Roche 1978, 67), into the later 1st century AD rather than the late Iron Age as originally proposed. Unlike the Ashville site there are no finewares amongst the Wyndyke assemblage on which to hinge any dating and no vessels that can be regarded as copies of imported forms (eg beakers and moulded platters). The first Romanised wares proper only appear in the early 2nd century and these are largely products of Oxfordshire industries.

Catalogue of illustrated sherds

***Bronze Age** (Fig. 3.1)*

1. Bodysherd from a Beaker with apparently randomly spaced fingernail impressions. Dark reddish-brown with a black interior. Fine grog tempering and sparse flint (GS). F5226, S5257.

2. Two rimsherds from a Beaker with fingernail impressed decoration set as horizontal lines. Fine mid brownish-orange grog-tempered ware (G00). F5279 (5278), S5021, redeposited.

3. Bodysherd from a Beaker with cord impressed decoration. Orange-brown in colour with grog tempering. F5553 (5569), redeposited.

4. Internally bevelled rim from a plain-walled small urn. Dark brownish-black exterior, pale brown interior. Sooting on the exterior. A fine, sandy matrix with sparse fragments of iron and limestone (fabric FI). The latter has mainly dissolved on the interior leaving fine voids. F5564 (5918).

***Early-middle Iron Age** (Fig. 3.2)*

5. Several sherds from a large bipartite jar with paired finger depressions on the carination. Very smooth, pale orange-brown surfaces with a grey core. The fine fabric contains sparse iron, fine limestone and probably alluvial shell (SL). F5024 (5023).

6. Large jar with an ovoid expanded rim. Orange with a grey core. Fabric L1. F5737 (5736).

7. Slack-sided jar, matt black in colour. Fabric S7. F5815 (5813), S6287.

8. Damaged rim sherd from a sharply carinated bowl with a black, finely burnished finish. Fabric S1. F5239 (5238), S5021.

9. Rim with fingertip decoration. Black in colour. Fabric L3 (slightly finer version). F5703 (5710), S5359.

10. Jar with slightly internally beaded rim and convex walls. Dark grey to red-brown in colour with a roughly smoothed exterior. Fabric IL1. F5007 (5006), S5359.

11. Small, simple rim jar/cup in a mid brown fine sandy, iron-rich ware. Fabric S2. Matt exterior. F5007 (5006), S5359.

12. Everted rim jar with a slightly ribbed exterior. Dark brown, slightly laminar fabric with sparse fine shell/limestone and iron. Fabric L3. F5553 (5569).

13. Carinated bodysherd decorated with finger depressions. Mid brown in colour with a grey core. Fabric L6. F5553 (5569).

14. Internally flanged vessel in a grey ware with an orange interior. Matt. Fabric L1. F5960 (5922).

15. Jar with internally expanded rim. Dark orange in colour with a grey core. Fabric L1. F5960 (5922).

16. Bodysherd with deeply impressed circular finger depressions. Fabric L1. F5960 (5922).

17. Jar with a heavy internally expanded rim with a slightly undulating upper surface marked by shallow finger impressions. Dark grey-black in colour. Fabric L1. F5960 (5922).

18. Bodysherd decorated with circular stab marks in a delimited panel-type design. Dark grey-black to brown in colour. Fabric S6. F5817 (5818).

19. Jar rim with probable notching on the rim edge. Orientation uncertain. Fabric L1. F5817 (5818).

20. Jar/bowl with vertical rim/neck expanding out into a wider body. Fabric L1. F5817 (5818).

21. Bodysherd decorated with small circular impressed rings delimited by an incised line. Fabric S1. Tr 29, F57 (58), S88.

***Early-middle Iron Age** (Fig. 3.3)*

22. Wide-mouthed jar/bowl with a slightly expanded rim. Patchy dark grey to brown with a reddish-orange core. Fabric I2. Matt, slightly rough exterior. External sooting below the rim. F5511 (5282).

23. Small simple rim bowl, mid reddish-brown to dark grey surfaces. The exterior is cursorily burnished and the interior smoothed. Fabric L1. F5511 (5282).

24. Jar with devolved shoulder carination. The vessel has a rough surface finish. Fabric L3. F5628 (5627), S6298.

25. Rim and two bodysherds from a globular-bodied jar with two countersunk handles. The exterior is slipped reddish-orange in colour originally with a burnished finish. Reddish-brown interior with a grey core. Sandy ware with fine alluvial shell. Fabric L2. F5624 (5620), S6298.

26. Bowl with a thick heavy base. Red-brown in colour with a smoothed burnished exterior and a smoothed interior. The sandy paste contains iron and alluvial shell. Fabric L4. Well F5664 (5889), S5664, Phase 4.

27. Large curved wall bowl in a matt dark grey-brown ware. Sandy ware with iron and sparse limestone/shell. Fabric L3. Well F5664 (5720), S5664.

28. Slack-sided jar. Red-brown to grey with a matt exterior with visible finger depressions around the rim zone where vessel has been shaped. Sandy ware with sparse shell/limestone. Fabric L2. Well F5664 (5719), S5664.

29. Small bowl with a simple, slightly beaded S-shaped rim. Burnished exterior. Sandy fabric with iron and sparse fine shell/limestone. Fabric L3. Well F5664 (5719).

30. Expanded rim jar/bowl with matt dark grey-brown surfaces. Fabric S2. Well F5664 (5718), S5664.

31. Lid with a well-burnished exterior. Black with a red-brown interior. Fabric S2. Well F5664 (5718), S5664.

32. Bodysherd with fingertip depressions on the carination. Orange-brown in colour, fabric L2. F5008 (5009), S6282.

33. Jar with finger depressions where shaped. Patchy red-orange to dark grey in colour with a rough surface finish. Fabric I2. F5008 (5009), S6282.

34. Ovoid jar with a slightly beaded rim. Smooth matt

exterior surface dark grey in colour. Fabric L7. Sooted exterior. F5008 (5009), S6282.

Early-middle Iron Age *(Fig. 3.4)*

35. Ovoid jar with a simple short rim. Matt with roughly smoothed external and internal surfaces. Fabric I2. Red-brown to dark grey in colour with slight external sooting. F6255 (6254), S6282.

36. Vertical-sided saucepan-style vessel with a smooth burnished exterior. Originally black but subsequently discoloured by staining. Fabric S1. F6255 (6254), S6282.

37. Two rimsherds and a bodysherd from a slack-sided jar. Dark grey-black in colour with a matt surface, sooted on the exterior. Fabric S1. F5372 (5364).

38. Ovoid jar with a simple incurved rim, black in colour. Fabric S5. F5372 (5364).

39. Ovoid jar with a short vertical rim. Reddish-brown ware containing sparse fine shell and rounded, probably alluvial limestone. Fabric L2. F5686 (5682), S6298.

40. Globular bowl with a well-burnished finish. Fabric S6. F5591 (5589), S6298.

41. Globular bowl in a dark brown ware with a smooth exterior, Fabric S6. F5591 (5589), S6298.

42. Globular bowl with a slightly beaded rim. Highly burnished exterior and smoothed interior surface. Patchy black to red-brown in colour. Fabric S4. (6275).

43. Globular bowl with a burnished exterior. Black to red-brown in colour. Fabric SL. F5740 (5743).

44. Simple rim globular bowl with a matt, smoothed exterior. Dark red-brown in colour. Fabric L2. F5270 (5269).

Roman *(Fig. 3.5)*

45. Wheelmade everted rim beaker in a fine dark grey ware. Fabric GREY4. F5359.

46. Bowl (Young 1977, form O42) in a fine dark orange ware with orange barbotine decoration. Fabric OXFOX. F5359.

47. Simple everted rim wheelmade jar. Dark grey-brown ware, slightly burnt with some sooting. Fabric GREY4. F5703 (5822), S5359.

48. Wheelmade dark orange jar. The rim appears to have been broken in antiquity and the resultant body fracture ground smooth, presumably to allow continued use of the container. Fabric OXFOX. F5703 (5822), S5359.

49. Wheelmade everted carinated dish, micaceous grey ware with a red core. Fabric GREY2. F5703 (5822), S5359.

50. Wheelmade carinated jar. Fabric OXFOX. F5703 (5822), S5359.

THE WORKED FLINT *by Philippa Bradley*

Introduction

A small assemblage consisting of 108 pieces of worked flint and four pieces of burnt unworked flint was recovered from the excavations. The flint was recovered from Iron Age and later features with generally only one or two pieces being recovered from each context.

Table 3.5 Worked flint assemblage composition

Flakes	Blades, blade-like flakes	Chips	Irregular waste	Cores	Retouched forms	Total	Burnt unworked flint
74*	10	5	1	4 (1 single platform, 1 multi-platform, 1 discoidal and 1 fragment)	14 (4 end and side scrapers, 3 end scrapers, 1 retouched flake, 1 microlith fragment, 1 retouched flake, 1 backed knife, 1 piercer, 3 miscellaneous pieces)	108	4

* including one core rejuvenation flake (face/edge)

The material is mostly gravel flint although a small quantity of chalk flint was identified. The flint was generally lightly corticated and some pieces were abraded and worn. The assemblage is summarised in Table 3.5, selected pieces are illustrated in Figure 3.6 and described in the catalogue of illustrated pieces. Further details of the flint assemblage may be found in the project archive.

Technology and dating

The assemblage consists of all elements of the reduction sequence, although some stages – chips and irregular waste, for example - seem to be under-represented. This may be due to post-depositional processes and collection methods. A few soft-hammer struck blades, blade-like flakes and flakes were recovered together with a single core rejuvenation flake and a broken microlith. The microlith is a small edge blunted type (Fig. 3.6, 1) and may be of later Mesolithic date, although these types occur throughout the Mesolithic (Pitts and Jacobi 1979, 169, fig. 5).

Both hard and soft hammers were used. Generally the flakes seem to have been hard-hammer struck with limited evidence for platform preparation. The cores recovered were used to produce unspecific flake removals (Table 3.5; Fig. 3.6, 4). Approximately 19.4% of the assemblage is burnt and 36.1% broken. This material would not be out of place within a Neolithic or Bronze Age context. The retouched forms present tend to confirm this date range. Unfortunately no diagnostic pieces were recovered which might have refined the dating further. Scrapers are the commonest type present in the assemblage (Table 3.5; Fig. 3.6, 2) and these tend to be neatly retouched on thin, often non-cortical blanks. The backed knife has fine invasive retouch (Fig. 3.6, 3) and may be of later Neolithic or early Bronze Age date. The edge of the knife is worn and gloss can be noted. The piercer is very crudely retouched and may be of middle or later Bronze Age date.

Discussion

The assemblage consists of essentially domestic items with scrapers dominating. Although most contexts produced only a limited number of pieces of flint there seems to be a concentration in the south-west part of the site perhaps indicating that this area was originally the focus for earlier prehistoric activity.

Mesolithic, Neolithic and Bronze Age flintwork has been found in the general area of the site (Holgate 1988). Excavations on the Ashville Trading Estate produced a

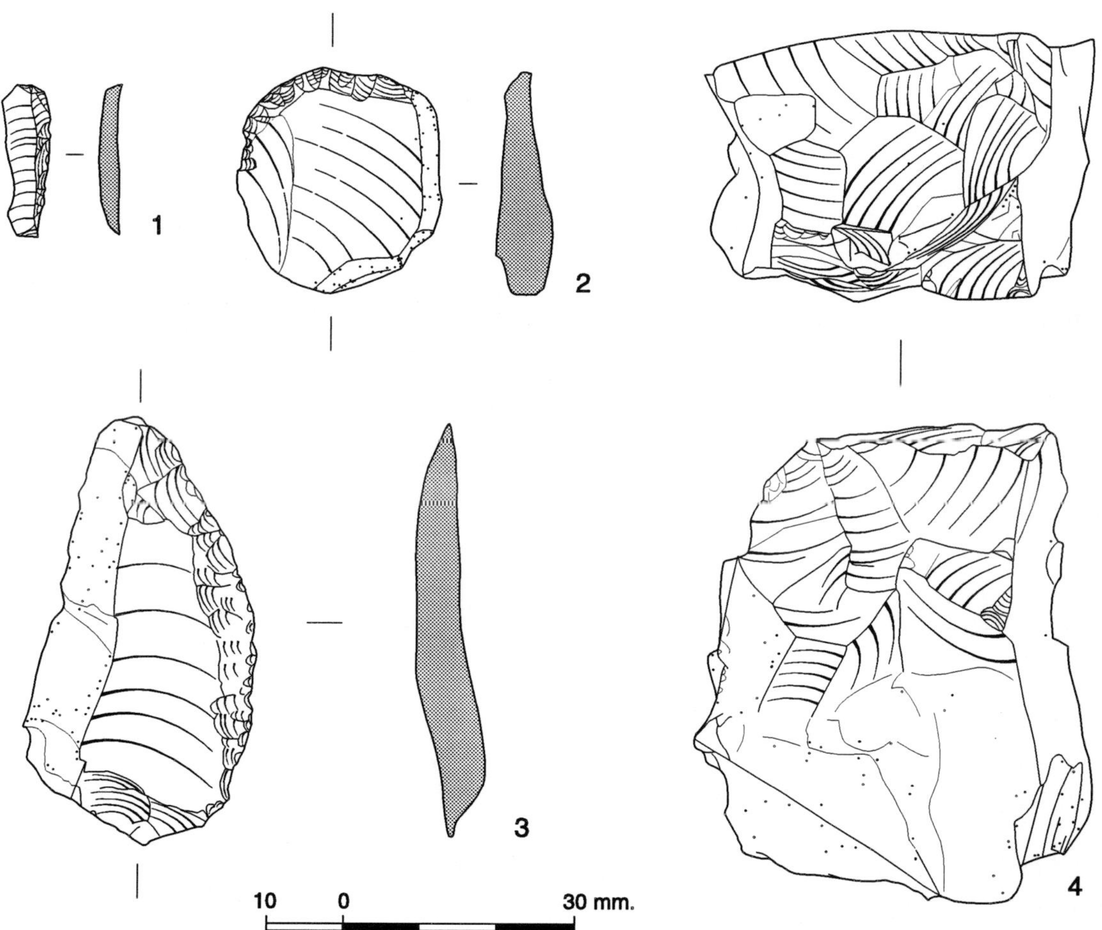

Figure 3.6 Worked Flint (1–4)

little material including arrowheads, axe fragments and debitage (Skellington 1978, 90–2, fig. 65) and a small quantity of flint, including an axe, was recovered from Claire Halpin's excavations at the former MG car factory (Halpin nd). A single broken and possibly burnt flake was recovered from a pit containing Grooved Ware found during the construction of the Abingdon Bypass (Balkwill 1978, 31, 33, fig. 29, no. 7). Mesolithic, Neolithic and Bronze Age flintwork has also been recovered from a series of excavations in the centre of Abingdon (Bradley in prep.), at Barton Court Farm (Whittle 1986), at Radley (Bradley 1999), Drayton (Holgate *et al.* in prep.) and various excavations at the Abingdon causewayed enclosure (Avery 1982). The material from Wyndyke Furlong compares well with these assemblages in terms of dating and composition.

Catalogue of illustrated pieces *(Fig. 3.6)*

Entries are ordered as follows: context number, brief description, weight (cores only) and small find number.

1. Context 5158. Edge blunted microlith. On small, broken bladelet, possibly later Mesolithic. Sf 5008.
2. Context 5360. End scraper. On side trimming flake. Neatly retouched, scraping angle 50-55°. Sf 5036.
3. Context 5533. Backed knife. Neat, invasively retouched example probably on chalk flint. Sf 5059.
4. Context 5558. Multi-platform flake core. Probably rejected because of the cherty nature of the flint. Weight 146 g. Sf 5123.

THE FIRED CLAY *by Alistair Barclay*

Introduction

The assemblage consists of 213 fragments weighing a total of 19.443 kg and includes an important group of Iron Age loomweights. Most of the fired clay was recovered from the fills of cut features belonging to the Iron Age settlement. None of the structural clay was recovered from *in situ* deposits. There was no evidence for metalworking debris (eg moulds or crucibles) or for salt containers (briquetage).

Method

The material was quantified by number of fragments and weight and a summary breakdown is given in Table 3.6. The fired clay occurs in a range of fabrics (A–F) which have been defined on the basis of principal inclusions. The fired clay was examined for evidence of wattle or other impressions, possible objects and structural pieces.

Fabrics

A - clay with rare large inclusions of rounded pebble gravel and angular limestone and some shell. (Used for loomweights, hearth clay and indeterminate fragments)

B - clay with very fine (1 mm) shell. (Indeterminate fragments)

C - clay with a wide range of inclusions including grog or angular clay pellets, small gravel and ironstone ooliths. (Indeterminate fragments)

D - clay with no significant inclusions. (Indeterminate, brick/tile-like fragment)

E - clay with coarse sand. (Miscellaneous object fragments, indeterminate fragments)

F - clay with calcareous grit (<2 mm). (Structural clay, indeterminate fragments)

Loomweights

The assemblage includes 23 fragments from at least nine different triangular loomweights of Iron Age form. Nearly all of these were recovered from pit context 5502. All of the loomweights are manufactured from fabric A, with the exception of a small fragment from context 5665 which is made from fabric F. Three of the weights

Table 3.6 Summary and quantification of all fired clay by type

Type	Number of fragments	Weight (kg)	Contexts	Comments
Loomweights	23	8.913	5314, 5352, 5502, 5665?	Triangular
Plate/brick/ tile like objects, misc. objects	18	2.981	5006, 5283, 5358–9, 5397, 5503, 5569, 5781, 5816, 6085	
Structural clay	37	0.965	5269, 5367, 5470, 5963	Fragments with wattle impressions
Hearth and oven	8	4.390	5502	Flattened clay lumps
Miscellaneous	127	2.194	5055, 5200, 5223, 5265, 5323, 5410, 5470, 5476, 5502–3, 5617, 5666, 5706, 5719–20, 5744, 5746, 5922	Mostly amorphous fragments.
Total	213	19.443		

Table 3.7 Comparison of all identified loomweights

Context	Sf No.	No.	Weight (g)	Fabric	Number of perforations	Completeness	Size	Thickness	Comment
5314		1	622	A	2/3?	3		50 mm	Many fresh breaks
5352	3202	1	259	A	?	5			
5502	5044	1	962	A	1	4		60 mm	
5502	5045	1	1300	A	1	1	150x150 x130 mm	40–60 mm	Complete weight
5502	5046	1	1200	A	1	1		95 mm	Part of massive weight
5502	5047	1	107	A	?	5			
5502	5049	1	1750	A	0	1		70 mm	
5502	5054	1	2000	A	0	1	190x190 x180 mm	60 mm	Almost complete
5502	5055	14	642	A	?	5			
5502	5056	1	71	A	1	5			
Total		23	8913						

Completeness: 1= >95%, 2= 75-95%, 3= 50-75%, 4= 25-50%, 5= <25%.

(SF 5045, 5049 and 5054) from context 5502 are either complete or almost so. Two other fragments (SF 5044 and context 5314) are from similar sized weights. Table 3.7 indicates the variation in their size and weight. Of the remainder, one fragment (SF 5046), also from 5502, is from a massive loomweight that has a thickness of 95 mm and is likely to come from a weight at the top end of the size range. The remaining three fragments are all too small to estimate actual size (see Table 3.7). At Gravelly Guy, where a large assemblage of loomweights was recovered, an attempt was made to divide the weights into large (1750-2100 g), medium (1375-1500 g) and small (300 g) categories (Barclay and Wait forthcoming). If the same classification is applied to the Wyndyke Furlong assemblage then two weights (SF5049, 5054) and two other fragments (SF5044, 5046) could be classed as large, while one other weight (SF5045) is of medium size. Most of the loomweights appeared to have at least one perforation, only one (context 5314) had two or three perforations, while two complete weights (SF 5049 and 5054) had no apparent perforations.

Plates and miscellaneous objects

A small number of contexts produced what could be object fragments (contexts 5283, 5397, 5503, 5569, 5665). Most of these fragments are relatively well-finished with recognisable surfaces, although they are generally too small or incomplete to identify as particular objects. Some fragments could be from loomweights, although it is thought that at least one fragment represents part of a clay plate-like object. A variety of plate-like objects have been found on sites in the Upper Thames and it is generally assumed that they were used as lids for large storage vessels or perhaps in the preparation of food (Barclay and Wait forthcoming). In addition, a number of brick-like or tile fragments were recovered from contexts 5006, 6085 (SF5112), 5781, 5816, 5358–9.

Structural clay

Thirty seven fragments of fired clay (0.965 kg) had wattle impressions most of which was manufactured from fabric F. Most pieces have only single wattle impressions or wattles that run in only one direction, although one piece from context 5367 has both vertical and horizontal impressions. This material is likely to derive from domestic oven structures or from burnt wall daub. None of this material was found *in situ*. Nearly all of this material (18 fragments, 687 g) was recovered from context 5367 (SF 5026–31). Other fragments of structural clay came from contexts 5269, 5473 and 5963.

Hearth/oven clay

Twenty two fragments weighing a total of 5028 g are from oven or hearth structures. Some of these lumps graded from oxidised to unburnt clay indicating firing *in situ*. Some fragments with straight or moulded edges and flattened surfaces could derive from oven structures. Most of this clay came from context 5502 (SF5048, 5051–2, 5057).

Miscellaneous

The majority of the fired clay (127 fragments, 2.194 kg) is amorphous and could mostly derive from ovens and hearths used for domestic and industrial activities. Some of it could represent the accidental burning of clayey soil. Most but not all of this material is fired a reddish-brown colour.

Discussion

The fired clay assemblage is fairly typical for an Iron Age settlement in the Oxford region of the Upper Thames Valley where loomweights and structural clay

Table 3.8 Ashville: Iron Age stone

Context	Sf No.	Description	Stone	Context type	Phasing
5	II	Burnt frag	Lower Greensand	Burial	Roman
13	-	Frag saddle quern	Corallian limestone	Penannular ditch	Period II
13	10	Frag saddle quern	Lower Calcareous Grit	Penannular ditch	Period II
30/4	12	Frag quern or rubber	Lower Greensand	Well	Roman
70	-	Rubber	Lower Greensand	Pit	Period I
82	9	Frag quern or rubber	Corallian limestone (gritty)	Well	Roman
129	16	Rubber	Corallian limestone	Well	Roman
135	8	Saddle quern	Corallian limestone	Pit	Period II
139	-	Saddle quern	Corallian limestone	Pit	Period II
281	-	2 frags rubber	Corallian limestone	Pit	Period II
313/2	-	Saddle quern	Lower Greensand	Pit	Period I
337	-	Frag	Lower Greensand	Pit	Period II
347	-	Saddle quern	Lower Calcareous Grit	Pit	Period II
445	-	Frag	Lower Greensand	Post pit	-
u/s	-	2 frags saddle quern	Lower Greensand	-	-

tend to be the dominant finds. The lack of briquetage, in particular that from Droitwich, is as expected as this material tends not to be found on sites to the south of the river Thames (Morris forthcoming; 1985). Loomweights, which are an indicator of textile production, were also found on the adjacent site at Ashville (Parrington 1978, 38) and have also been found at the Vineyard (Barclay in prep.). Of the remainder, the structural clay and so-called hearth clay provide indirect evidence for domestic ovens, while some of the structural clay could derive from burnt daub walls. One pit (5502) produced a significant quantity of fired clay that included hearth clay and loomweights as well as other amorphous fragments.

THE WORKED STONE *by Fiona Roe*

Introduction

The stone assemblage from Wyndyke Furlong consists of pieces from ten contexts. There are five worked objects, while fragments from another five contexts are of quern materials, although on these working traces no longer survive. Burnt stone amounted to 5.526 kg.

The Iron Age

There are pieces of stone from four Iron Age contexts. Three fragments from a saddle quern made from Lower Greensand came from context 5023, a posthole dated to the early/middle Iron Age. The fragments were no doubt used as postpacking. The greensand could have been obtained locally, from around Culham, at a distance of some 5 kilometres (3.2 miles). Another weathered piece of the same variety of stone (5142) came from a middle Iron Age context, ring gully 5021. The same ring gully also yielded a well-worn hammerstone of quartzitic sandstone (context 5271). This material could also have been collected locally, from pebbles in Pleistocene deposits such as the gravels of the Summer-town/Radley terrace (Pocock 1926, 136). A dual purpose hammerstone and grindingstone made from a quartzite pebble came from a middle Iron Age pit (context 5637).

A further five finds which are unphased or from Roman contexts seem likely also to belong to the Iron Age occupation. These include a third hammerstone utilising a quartzite pebble (context 5558). There are two further fragments of Lower Greensand (contexts 5199, 5558). Another local material is Corallian limestone, available from 3.2 km (2 miles) away (Arkell 1947, 91, fig. 13; see also Geological Survey Sheet 253) which was used for a saddle quern (context 29/22). It is unlikely that sarsen came from very far away either. Although this was a good material for querns, only two burnt lumps (from context 29/44) survive, and these may have been re-used as hearthstones. Nearly all the burnt stone consists of Corallian limestone, but 16.8% is Lower Calcareous Grit, also from the Corallian, while some 5% was found to be fragments from burnt quartzite pebbles.

The Roman period

Only one Roman context has yielded quern material. There are small fragments of Niedermendig lava from ditch 3204 which could have belonged either to a quern or a millstone.

Discussion

The finds described above are best viewed in the wider context of the worked stone previously recorded in 1974 – 6 at the Ashville Trading Estate (Parrington 1978, 88). These earlier finds are summarised in Tables 3.8–3.11, together with the 1994 worked stone.

The Iron Age

It can be seen from Tables 3.8 and 3.9 that in the Iron Age there was consistent use of local materials for saddle querns at both excavated sites. Fragments of Lower Greensand came from eleven contexts, while both Lower Calcareous Grit and limestone (often gritty) from the Corallian came from a further ten contexts. (In four cases

Table 3.9 Wyndyke Furlong: Iron Age stone

Context	Sf No.	Description	Stone	Context type	Phasing
29/22	29/3	Frag saddle quern	Corallian limestone	Top of waterhole	Uncertain
29/44	-	2 burnt lumps	Sarsen	Ditch	Uncertain
5023	5024	3 frags saddle quern	Lower Greensand	PH	EIA/EMIA
5142	5121	Frag	Lower Greensand	Ring gully	MIA
5199	5118	Frag	Lower Greensand	-	-
5271	5116	Hammerstone	Quartzitic sandstone	Ring gully	MIA
5558	5117	Hammerstone	Quartzite	PH	Uncertain
5558	5120	Frag	Lower Greensand	PH	Uncertain
5637	5112	Hammerstone/grindingstone	Quartzite	Pit	MIA

it has been assumed that finds from Roman contexts have been redeposited).

It is now known that by the Middle Iron Age the local greensand and Corallian sandstone or limestone were both very much traditional quern materials, since they had been in use since the earlier prehistoric period. A rubber of sandy limestone from the Lower Calcareous Grit was recorded from the nearby Abingdon causewayed enclosure (Case and Whittle 1982, 42), while another came from a Grooved Ware pit (3831) at Barrow Hills, Radley (Roe 1999). The Lower Greensand from Culham was in use from at least the Bronze Age, as it has occurred in early prehistoric contexts at Yarnton Floodplain (Roe in prep. a), and also in a pit of probable Beaker date at Gravelly Guy, Stanton Harcourt (Roe forthcoming a). Sarsen and pebbles from Pleistocene deposits were also acquired locally for use at Wyndyke Furlong, and again artefacts made from both these materials had a very long period of use.

In this setting it is somewhat difficult to interpret the find of a rotary quern fragment made from Upper Old Red Sandstone which was found at the Ashville Trading Estate in pit 55. This pit was tentatively attributed to Iron Age period II (De Roche 1978, 47), and the quern might therefore appear to provide evidence for the early use at Ashville of rotary querns made from imported materials. However only two sherds of Iron Age pottery were found in this pit (Ashville Trading Estate archive), so it seems a real possibility that they were redeposited, and that the quern fragment belongs with the Roman occupation at the site, discussed below.

Burnt stone is common on Oxfordshire Iron Age sites, as for instance at Watkins Farm, Northmoor, where a large quantity of burnt limestone was noted (Allen 1990a, 94), so Wyndyke Furlong is no exception in this respect.

The apparent exclusive use of local materials for saddle querns at the Abingdon Trading Estate would seem to confirm the original excavator's suggestion that this was a self-sufficient community (Parrington 1978, 38). However it is somewhat unusual to find no imported saddle quern materials on an Iron Age site in the Upper Thames Valley. Other local sites, investigated since the Ashville Trading Estate excavations took place, have nearly all produced quern fragments of May Hill sandstone, which were brought into the area from up to 53 miles away. These sites include ones relatively close to Wyndyke Furlong, such as Abingdon Vineyard (Roe forthcoming b), Watkins Farm, Northmoor (Allen 1990a, 94), Gravelly Guy, Stanton Harcourt (Bradley *et al.* forthcoming; Roe forthcoming a), Mingies Ditch, Hardwick-with-Yelford (Allen and Robinson 1993, 79), Deer Park Road, Witney (Roe 1995, 84) and Cresswell Field, Yarnton (Roe in prep. b). These sites all tend to have saddle querns of Lower Greensand and Lower Calcareous Grit as well. Deer Park Road, Witney is an exception, though here the Lower Greensand featured as a possible temper for some of the pottery (Timby 1995, 80). There are just a few sites without imported saddle

Table 3.10 Ashville: Roman Stone

Context	Sf No.	Description	Stone	Context type	Phasing
I	II	Counter	Fine-grained limestone	Burial	Roman
30/4	-	Rubber or polisher	Quartzitic sandstone	Well	R/B
55	11	Frag rotary quern	Upper Old Red Sandstone, quartz conglomerate	Pit	IA period II (?)
450	-	Frag rotary quern	Millstone Grit	PH	Roman
Unreg	-	Frag whetstone	Kentish Rag	-	-
Q 1	TS	Frag rotary quern	Millstone Grit	-	-
Q2	TS	Frag rotary quern	Upper Old Red Sandstone, sandstone	-	-
Q3	TS	4 frags rotary quern or millstone	Millstone Grit	Topsoil	u/s

Table 3.11 Wyndyke Furlong: Roman Stone

Context	Sf No.	Description	Stone	Context type	Phasing
3204	-	12 small fragments	Niedermendig lava	Ditch 3204	Early 2nd C AD

quern materials. Those at Whitehouse Road, Oxford (Mudd 1993, 66) and the Oxford University Science Area (Parkinson *et al.* 1996, 48) are both represented by small samples. Only at Farmoor do the finds of Iron Age stone compare well with those from Wyndyke Furlong, as indeed does the pottery (Lambrick and Robinson 1979, 59; Timby 1995, 81).

The explanation for the probable absence of imported saddle quern material at Wyndyke Furlong may be a question of status. The nearest Iron Age site, Abingdon Vineyard, is undoubtedly of higher status, and so might be expected to have received prestigious imported goods, which in the middle Iron Age included May Hill sandstone (Roe forthcoming b). However the Vineyard is probably on the eastern edge of the May Hill sandstone distribution, and a lower status site in the same area, and one already well supplied with local quern materials, could have missed out on imported goods. By contrast, at the Vineyard, both Lodsworth stone and Millstone Grit seem to have been acquired during the middle Iron Age for rotary querns (Roe forthcoming b), although rotary querns made from Upper Old Red Sandstone do not occur here before the middle Roman period.

The Roman period

Turning to the Roman period (Tables 3.10 and 3.11) an entirely different range of quern materials is found, all imported to the site. Two of these, Millstone Grit and Niedermendig lava, were demonstrably used for rotary querns, and probably also the Old Red Sandstone, which occurred unstratified. Kentish Rag from the Maidstone area (again unstratified but assumed to be Roman) was used for a whetstone. All these materials occur commonly on Roman sites in Oxfordshire. All three quern materials, for instance, were found at Mill Street Wantage (Roe 1996, 152). At Asthall there were querns of Millstone Grit and Old Red Sandstone, and whetstones of Kentish Rag (Roe 1997, 100). All four imported materials occurred again at Alchester (Roe forthcoming c). At Abingdon Vineyard the main Roman quern material appears to have been the Lodsworth stone from Sussex, but Upper Old Red Sandstone and Niedermendig lava were also found, and again a whetstone of Kentish Rag (Roe forthcoming b).

The two contrasting groups of finds from the two separate periods at Wyndyke Furlong demonstrate how different quern materials were adopted once the new technology associated with rotary querns had arrived. In Oxfordshire the use of rotary querns led to the importation of various types of stone, all different from those previously in use. The period of change must have taken place sometime between the late middle Iron Age and the late Iron Age. Further excavations on sites dating to this time range, absent at Wyndyke Furlong, could cast more light on Iron Age trading activities at this interesting juncture in time.

THE SMALL FINDS *by Kate Atherton*

Introduction

A total of twenty objects were recovered during the archaeological investigations at Wyndyke Furlong. The assemblage consists of the following categories of material: copper alloy (three items), iron (eight items), bone (six objects), shale (one object), leather (one fragment) and slate (one object). Each item has been catalogued, grouped together by material and discussed by function where possible. The catalogue entries for the objects are listed in context order.

Copper alloy

Three strips of copper alloy were found, none of which are complete and all of which are in a poor condition. Precise identification, therefore, is not possible and any interpretation must remain speculative. The better preserved strip, SF 5095 from a middle Iron Age ditch, survives to a length of 70 mm. The shank has a rectangular section and it twists along its length. One end terminates in a point while the other end expands but is broken. It is possible that this object could be the handle from an item such as a spoon (Cunliffe 1971, 112, fig. 47 no. 122) or the shank from a pin (Coles 1987, 71, fig. 3.12 no. E67). The remaining strips show no distinctive features and can only be classified as miscellaneous objects.

(Not illustrated)

Strip. Copper alloy. Context 5573, SF 5062. L: 18 mm; W: 11 mm; Th: 1 mm. Irregularly shaped fragment of copper alloy sheet. One side flat with raised area of copper alloy on the other side. From primary fill of middle Iron Age pit.

Strip. Copper alloy. Context 5704, SF 5074. L: 17 mm; W: 2 mm. Round section. Possible remains of two tiny projections of copper alloy, one towards the centre and one towards the end, possibly to attach it to something. Curved to form a hooked shape. Both ends broken. From top fill of a late 1st/2nd C ditch. Same ditch as shale vessel fragment.

Strip. Copper alloy. Context 5813, SF 5095. L: 70 mm; W: 3 mm. Curved along its length with one end tapering to a point. Bent so length approximate. From middle Iron Age ditch.

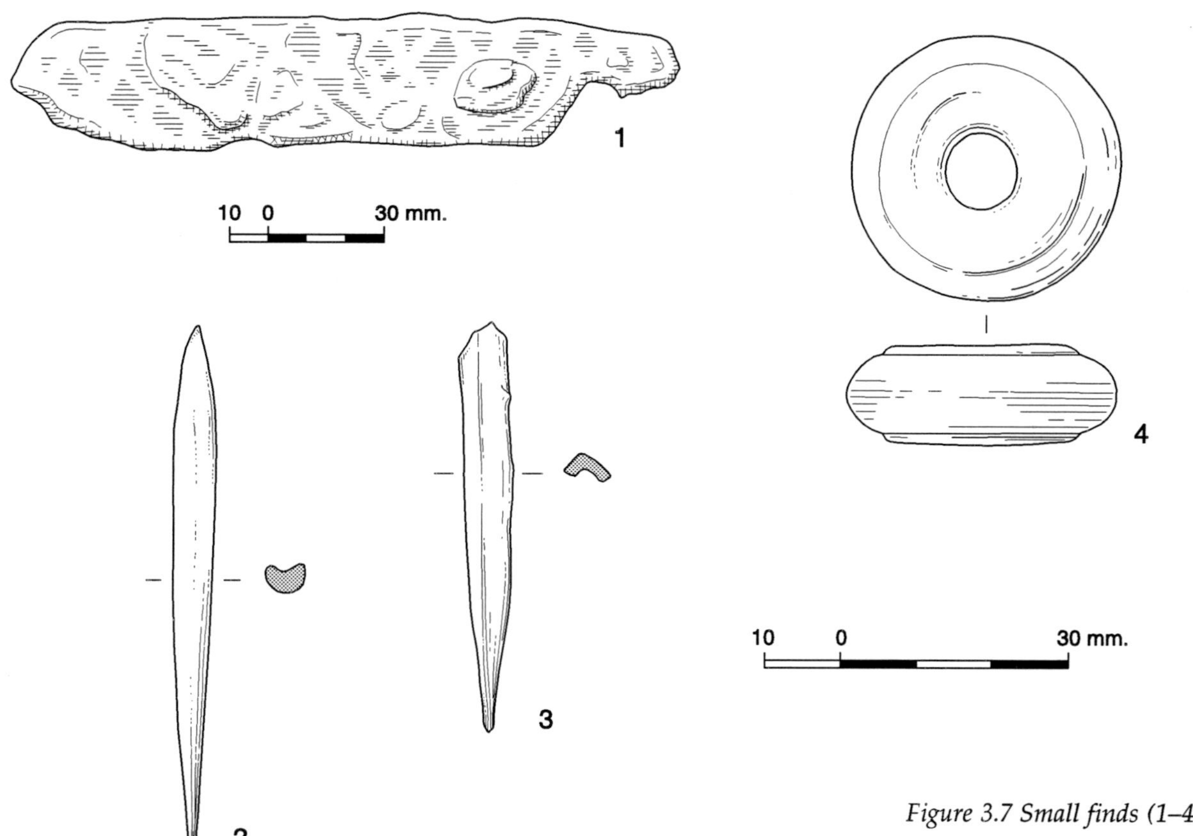

Figure 3.7 Small finds (1–4)

Iron

Eight iron objects were found during the excavations. These consist of a knife blade, five nails, an angled strip and a post-medieval horseshoe. A complete blade (SF 2; Fig. 3.7, 1) was recovered from an undated ditch. This is the blade of a whittle tang knife which has a tang, now broken, that extends the line of the top of the blade. The tang would have been inserted inside a handle made from another material such as bone or wood. The top of the blade and the cutting edge are straight for most of the length until they taper in a shallow curve to form the blade tip. This type of knife can be found in contexts that date throughout the Roman period (Manning 1985, 116–17, plate 55, Q58).

Five nails were recovered from three contexts (contexts 5014, 5812 and three from context 5818) but only one is complete. Four of the nails, including the complete nail from context 5818, have rectangular shanks with small, flat flanged heads and all have incomplete lengths that range from *c* 55 mm to *c* 65 mm. The nail from context 5812 (SF 5092) is distinguished from the other four nails by its circular shank and its twisted head but it is unlikely that it was anything other than a nail or structural rivet. A strip of iron with a rectangular section (SF 5001) was found in context 5035. There is a tight bend in the strip but this appears to have been caused by damage and not to have been related to its original function. It is, therefore, possible that the strip is also part of a nail shank.

The eighth iron object is a complete horseshoe from an evaluation trench (context 23/03). The horseshoe has a plain outline, wide webs and no trace of a heel with calkins. It has six rectangular holes, three in each branch, which are set within a fullered groove which runs around the outer edge of the shoe. The fragmentary remains of a nail survive in one hole. This type of shoe was introduced in the 14th century and remains unchanged in form at the present day (Goodall 1990, 1056). The fullered groove is a characteristic found in horseshoes from the 17th century onwards.

Fig. 3.7, 1

Whittle tang knife. Iron. Context 3216 SF 2. L: 172 mm; W: 36 mm; Th: 5 mm. Complete blade of whittle tang knife with slightly arched top and broken tang continuing the line of the top of the blade. The top of the blade falls in a shallow curve to the tip. Bottom of blade edge straight and then tapers towards tip which is broken. From a shallow ditch, probably a drain. Roman.

(Not illustrated)

Horseshoe. Iron. Context 23/03. L: 120 mm; W: 112 mm; Th: 6 mm. Complete. Wide web: 28–32 mm. Six rectangular holes: 8 x 5 mm. The holes lie in a fullered groove, *c* 4 mm wide, around the outer edge. Fragment of horseshoe nail in one hole. No evidence for calkins or heel. Plain outline. Post-medieval.

Strip. Iron. Context 5035, SF 5001 L: 50 mm; W: 7 mm. Strip of iron that turns back on itself at a tight angle for a length of 33 mm. Rectangular cross-section. From posthole cluster (6314) of uncertain date. Possibly a bent nail shank/rod. Wood remains around angle.

Nail. Iron. Context 5283, SF 5014. L: 55 mm. Near complete nail with small circular flat flanged head and broken tip. From top fill of mid to late 1st C ditch. Like polished bone.

Nail. Iron. Context 5812, SF 5092. L: 64 mm. Possible nail with flat round twisted head and straight shank before bent end. Tip is broken. From middle Iron Age gully/ enclosure ditch.

Three nails. Iron. Context 5818, SF 5091. One complete nail, one near complete nail, with bends at right angles, lengths: *c* 56 mm and *c* 60 mm. Other fragment is nail head. All have thin shanks and small flat circular flanged heads. From middle Iron Age pit.

Bone

The investigations produced six bone objects, four of which can be identified as tools that are probably associated with textile manufacture. The two remaining bones are highly polished and possibly served as more general 'all-purpose' tools but also, most probably, within a textile context. The four tools were all recovered from middle Iron Age features.

A double-pointed bone implement (SF 5002, Fig. 3.7, 2) was found in context 5052. The tool is made from a splinter of bone that has been finely worked along its length. One end forms a sharp point with a triangular section. The body of the object arches in the centre before flattening and expanding towards the other end to form a wider and blunter point. The upper surface is polished through use. This object is similar to tools found on Saxon sites that are also double-pointed and polished and are interpreted as thread pickers used for delicate textile work (Miles 1986, 5:A8 fig. 93.6–8). It is unlikely that SF 5002 is Saxon because the shape of the object differs from the normal regular cigar-shape of Saxon thread pickers and pin beaters and it is not as finely worked. However, it is possible that a similar function was intended for the point. Excavations of the Iron Age settlement at Meare Village East in Somerset produced a splinter of a similar size that was also pointed at both ends although the Wyndyke Furlong find is a more delicate example (Coles 1987, 53, fig. 3.3, B9). Coles argues that such points could have had a variety of purposes, including fine work associated with textile manufacture and, less likely, use as an eating implement (Coles 1987, 53).

A bone awl (Fig. 3.7, 3) was recovered from middle Iron Age context 5312. The awl is similar to Danebury Class 3 awls that are made from bone splinters which vary in size and character (Sellwood 1984, 387). The common factor is a long needle-like point that is rounded in section. The point almost invariably has the highest polish and is usually quite sharp although sometimes worn to a rounded profile. They are in general found less commonly than gouges (see below). The general function of an awl is to pierce or bore a hole in a softer substance and Class 3 awls in particular are most frequently associated with leatherworking or densely woven fabrics where they would not leave a large hole. The Wyndyke Furlong awl is made from a splinter of a sheep metatarsal and the tip is broken through use.

The Wyndyke Furlong excavations produced a particularly fine example of a complete spindle whorl (SF 5096, Fig. 3.7, 4). The whorl is bun-shaped, lathe-turned and decorated with concentric lines and is highly polished through wear. Spindle whorls, used in the spinning process, were made from a variety of materials, including stone, glass, shale, pottery and bone and it is likely that the material was unimportant. The Wyndyke Furlong whorl is comparable in size and style to whorls from Meare Village East, made from rock (Coles 1987, 166, fig. 3.70 no. W174) and shale (Coles 1987, 158, fig. 3.66 no. W15). However, the few bone spindle whorls made during the Iron Age were normally made from bovine femurs which is a spongy material. It is more likely that the Wyndyke Furlong whorl is made from antler which became a popular material for whorls during the Roman period. Antler provided a solid tissue that encouraged incised decoration which usually took the form of turned rings on discoid or sub-spherical whorls (MacGregor 1985, 86, fig. 101, nos 7–8). It is, therefore, more likely that the whorl is late Iron Age or Roman than middle Iron Age. The large size of the whorl suggests that it could have been used for spinning coarser yarns or for plying multiple threads.

Gouges are commonly found on Iron Age settlement sites and are often made of sheep tibia, as is the example from Wyndyke Furlong (context 5924). Gouges are characterised by long, pointed terminals, created by slicing the end of the bone along its length and hollowing out the inside of the bone, leaving raised flanges at either side. The extreme tip of the gouge is broken but would have been a thin, flat point. There is a high degree of polish on the tip, particularly on the underside, and an overall sheen caused by wear. The butt of the gouge can often be pierced but the butt of the Wyndyke Furlong example appears to have been trimmed. Several functions have been suggested for gouges and interpretations include spoons, pins, skewers, weaving shuttles and a general all-purpose use. However, the fact that a high proportion were made from particular bones and have a characteristic shape suggests a specific purpose and it is possible that they acted as pin-beaters in the weaving process (Sellwood 1984, 385, fig. 7.33, 3.101–3.116, 387).

Polished and grooved bone implements are common finds from excavations of Iron Age settlements but their purpose remains unclear. The Wyndyke Furlong investigations recovered two such bones, from contexts 5283 (dating from the mid to late 1st century) and 5598 (dating from the late 1st century to 2nd century).

The object from context 5598 is a polished sheep metapodial with transverse grooves and a thinning of the bone on opposite sides of the shaft near the distal end. Similar objects have been found at Meare Village East (Coles 1987, 145–50, fig. 361), at Farmoor (Lambrick and Robinson 1979, 55), at Barton Court (Miles 1986, 5:A5) and at Ashville (Parrington 1978, 81-83). It was suggested that the polished Farmoor and Ashville bones were used for weaving or leather-working. The cow metacarpal from Wyndyke Furlong (context 5283) has a central band of polished surface but, unlike the polished sheep metacarpal from Ashville (Parrington 1978, 81–83, fig. 61, no. 39), there are no remains of grooves. The Ashville example was thought possibly to be a pin beater but the Wyndyke Furlong example does not have the same defined grooves across the width of the bone and it would be expected that the knobbed ends of the bones would be a hindrance. A similar ox metacarpal was found at Meare Village East (Coles 1987, 52, fig. 3.2, B33). The polishing is clearly the result of constant handling and use but, although these are common finds and are thought to be connected with the weaving process, a more precise function is not known.

(Fig. 3.7, 2)

Double-ended point. Bone. Context 5052, SF 5002. L: 70 mm; W: 5 mm at widest point. Bone splinter tapering to a sharp point at one end, sub-square in section. The other end is flattened to form an expanded point. Polished on the upper surface. From middle Iron Age house gully.

(Fig. 3.7, 3)

Awl. Bone. Context 5312. L: 54 mm. Awl made from a splinter of a sheep's metatarsal with a needle like point, circular in section, broken at the tip. From middle Iron Age pit (also contained whole pot 5313).

(Fig. 3.7, 4)

Spindle whorl. Bone. Context 5825, SF 5096. D: 36 mm; Th: 11 mm; D of inner hole: 10 mm. Complete bun-shaped spindle whorl, facetted with concentric line decoration, areas round the central perforation are highly polished. From middle Iron Age pit.

(Not illustrated)

Gouge. Bone. Context 5924. L: 90 mm. Long pointed terminal with raised flanges at either side. The tip of the tool is missing, the upper end of the gouge is also damaged. The object is polished all over. From middle Iron Age pit. Sheep tibia.

Object. Bone. Context 5283. L: 164 mm. Cow metacarpal, highly polished around the centre of the bone for a band of *c* 90 mm. Particularly polished on the upper side. From top fill of mid to late 1st C ditch (like nail).

Object. Bone. Context 5598. L: 92 mm. Grooved and polished sheep metapodial. Transverse grooves and a thinning of the bone appear on opposite sides of the shaft near the distal end. The proximal end is missing. The metapodial is polished all over. From late 1st to 2nd C ditch.

Other material

Objects made from other materials consist of a fragment from a shale bowl and a scrap of leather. A post-medieval slate pencil, clearly an intrusive find, is not considered further.

The shale vessel fragment was recovered from the same ditch, dated to the 1st to 2nd century AD, as SF 5074, a strip of copper alloy (see above). The small fragment (20 g) is from the body and base of a lathe-turned bowl that is decorated with incised concentric lines. The considerable skill required to produce shale vessels was developed during the Iron Age period and a similar fragment of bowl was found at Meare Village East (Coles 1987, 135, fig. 3.57, K37). Shale vessels are more frequently found at Roman sites and a comparable fragment from the bottom of a shale vessel occurred at Silchester (Lawson 1976, 257, fig. 7, no. 73). This bowl also has a foot ring and horizontal grooves with rounded ridges between them, and thick shale for the base and thinner material for the vessel walls. Lawson suggests that an early Roman date may be indicated by these features but that it may be difficult to date shale vessels in such a manner because these features are so suited to the material (Lawson 1976, 260). However, the date of the feature that produced the Wyndyke Furlong shale fragment would support the theory.

A fragment from a sheet of leather (SF 5073) was found in context 5701, the fill of a middle Iron Age pit. The fragment has no distinguishing features nor defined edges and, therefore, the fragment can only be classified as a scrap of leather of uncertain purpose.

(Not illustrated)

Vessel. Shale. Context 5822. L: 80 mm; Wt: 20 g. Body fragment from a shale shallow bowl, decorated with incised concentric lines. Beginnings of base. From 1st –2nd C AD ditch. Same ditch as SF 5074 ca strip. Thickness of shale: 6-8 mm.

Sheet. Leather. Context 5701, SF 5073 . L: 54 mm; W: 30 mm. Scrap of leather sheet. From middle Iron Age pit.

Pencil. Slate. Context 29/58. One end has been sharpened. From late Iron Age ditch.

Discussion

The assemblage of metal finds is small and not of a high quality. The amount of metalwork that might be expected from a large settlement, especially nails, is absent. This may suggest that the soil conditions prevent the preservation of copper alloy and iron and only provide a glimpse of what might have existed at the site. Shale and organic materials, such as bone and leather, survive in a better condition although the assemblage is again too small to draw any useful conclusions about activity at the site. The bone objects support the theory that textile manufacture, and possibly leatherworking, took place at the settlement during the Iron Age period and into the Roman period, but the finds appear to be randomly scattered around the settlement and to cover a long period of time.

THE METAL-WORKING DEBRIS *by Chris Salter*

The evidence

Just over one kilogram of material was examined, most of which, 76% by weight, can be attributed to iron-working (Table 3.12). It is likely that most of the remaining material, 21% by weight, a variety of low-density slag type is also the result of iron-working activity, even though such material can be generated by a variety of high temperature processes. Just over half the material was in the form of fragments of smithing hearth bottoms, together with a few nearly complete examples. One flake of hammer scale was also recovered. Some undiagnostic ironworking slag together with low density slag came from middle Iron Age contexts, whereas the smithing hearth bottom material was confined to the Romano-British period. Although there is evidence of later metal-working from other areas in the vicinity of Abingdon, there is no reason to suppose that the undated material was not derived from two short lived episodes of ironworking working in the immediate vicinity during the middle Iron Age and Romano-British periods.

The wider context

Unfortunately, the reports on metal-working debris (Cleere 1978) from Ashville Trading Estate (Parrington 1978) and Barton Court Farm (Miles 1986) do not give weights of material recovered. Therefore, it is difficult to compare these sites with Wyndyke Furlong. The impression given, however, is that the amounts of slag were similar to that recovered at Wyndyke Furlong. Rather larger amounts of material were recovered from the Vineyard site where 54 kg of unsorted 'slag' has been recovered from Iron Age, Romano-British and undated features (Salter, work in progress).

Very little is known about Iron Age and Romano-British iron production and working in the Abingdon-Oxford area. It is not clear whether there was any iron smelting activity in the clay vales between the Chilterns and the Cotswolds, or around the Greensand outliers, although there are useable iron ores available. There is undated evidence of smelting in the Otmoor area (M. Farley, pers. comm.), and in the Elsfield area. The evidence of ironworking from the local excavated sites is in desperate need of re-examination in the light of modern excavations and experimental reconstruction elsewhere in the country. Taking the published evidence at face value, the iron economy in the Abingdon area for the Iron Age and Romano-British periods was entirely dependent on iron supplied from outside the immediate vicinity.

There is evidence for a limited amount of iron forging activity, but no evidence of iron production (smelting). However, Cleere, although not giving a weight, seemed to be impressed by the size of the slag cake from the late Iron ditch (103) at the Ashville Trading Estate. Such a piece of slag could be the result of iron smelting using non-slag tapping technology. It could be argued, if one follows the model proposed by Hingley (1997), that the location of this piece in an enclosure ditch close to its south-east facing entrance suggests that it might be connected with smelting. This suggests, following African ethnographic evidence, that the iron-smelting process was often strongly linked with regeneration, and that such eastern/south-eastern doorways and enclosure openings were also associated with the rising sun, rebirth and regeneration. In the case of Wyndyke Furlong there was no similar correlation between the metalworking debris and the archaeological features. However, the possible presence of small amounts of iron smelting slag which could easily dismissed simply as smithing debris, must be considered when assessing Iron Age metal-working in the region and particularly when such deposits are associated with enclosure boundaries and enclosure entrances.

Table 3.12 Weight of metal-working debris types by period.

Period	Smithing Hearth bottom	Smithing Hearth bottom frags	Undiagnostic Iron-working slag	Low density slag	Hammer scale	Fired clay
MIA			99.4	64.0		
Romano-British	594.0			40.3		
Undated			4.5	12.1	0.1	
Unknown		124.0	76.5	130.0		1.0

All weights given in grammes.

Chapter 4: The Human, Plant and Animal Remains

THE HUMAN REMAINS *by Angela Boyle*

Three fragments of human bone were initially misidentified as animal bone. All three are skull fragments although they derive from separate contexts.

Context 5139: a single skull fragment from the top fill of a middle Iron Age ring gully (5141, Structure 5021, Fig 2.14); bone is parietal fragment (possibly left posterior) possibly from an adult individual; possible wormian bone present; the broken edges are completely unworn.

Context 5434: a single skull fragment from an undated pit or posthole; bone is a parietal fragment from an adult; the broken edges are completely unworn.

Context 5569: a single skull fragment from the fill of a large pit dating to the middle Iron Age; bone is occipital fragment from an adult individual; the broken edges are completely unworn.

Discussion

Three deposits of disarticulated human skull were recovered. One of these (5139) was from a structural feature, the fill of a ring gully (5021), the second was recovered from the surface of a posthole or pit which was part of posthole cluster 6314, while the third derived from the middle fill (5569) of a large pit (5553). This pit fill also contained 22 fragmented vertebrae of a cattlebeast and it has been suggested that this deposit may be of symbolic or ritual significance (see below). The pit also contained a fragment of copper alloy strip (see chapter 3), an everted rim jar and a carinated body sherd decorated with finger-tip impressions (see chapter 3).

Human remains were also recovered during the adjacent excavations at Ashville. They consisted of an articulated burial from pit 62 and disarticulated fragments: two subadult bones from pit 69, a tibia fragment from pit 72, an incomplete occipital bone from pit 79, a lumbar vertebra from pit 388 and a femur fragment from ditch 392 in association with a partial dog skeleton (Edwards 1978, 92; Wilson *et al.* 1978, 125).

A number of other Iron Age settlements have produced evidence of what might superficially appear to be casual treatment of dead bodies. Isolated human bones are frequently found in rubbish deposits and articulated parts of human carcasses have been found in pits along with other occupation debris. Other examples from the Upper Thames include Mount Farm, Berinsfield (Barclay and Lambrick 1995) and Gravelly Guy, Stanton Harcourt (Lambrick *et al.* forthcoming) where 65 deposits of disarticulated human bone fragments were recovered. The fact that these deposits appear in features which are very much an integral part of the settlements is noteworthy and emphasises the juxtaposition of the living and the dead which is now regularly seen as a defining characteristic of the Iron Age (Fitzpatrick and Morris 1994, x). Recent work has focussed on the formation of such deposits and it has been argued that they are in fact highly structured (Hill 1995).

The presence of only a single pit burial at Ashville and their absence at Wyndyke Furlong is also worthy of comment. At the latter site a total of 51 out of 77 pits were excavated and we might therefore conclude that the absence of storage-pit inhumations is genuine. The recently excavated middle Iron Age cemetery at Yarnton was located on the periphery of the settlement; within the settlement pit burials were absent and there was a general paucity of disarticulated fragments (Hey *et al.* 1999). The cemetery at Yarnton is not unique and other examples include Cockey Down, near Salisbury (Trust for Wessex Archaeology 1996) and Suddern Farm (Cunliffe 1996). One might therefore reasonably suggest that the absence of pit burials and disarticulated fragments on settlement sites could be indicative of the presence of dedicated cemeteries on their peripheries.

MACROSCOPIC PLANT AND INVERTEBRATE REMAINS *by Jenny Robinson*

Introduction

In order to recover waterlogged remains, bulk samples were taken during the excavations at Wyndyke Furlong from middle Iron Age well 5664 and the middle to late Iron Age waterhole or well 29/9. Samples from other deposits were floated onto a 0.5 mm mesh to recover charred plant remains.

Methods and results

A 1 kg subsample of the two bottom-most waterlogged samples from each well was sieved down to 0.2 mm and sorted. Waterlogged plant remains were entirely absent from one well (Samples 5028 and 5029). The other two samples (Samples 29/5 and 29/6) contained numerous well-preserved waterlogged seeds, some charred plant remains, mollusc shells and rather badly preserved insect remains, and so they were sorted under a binocular microscope. The plant and mollusc remains were identified in full, the results being listed in Tables 4.1–4.3.

The 45 flots from dated contexts were fully sorted under a binocular microscope for charred plant remains other than charcoal. These were identified. 25 of the 30 early to middle Iron Age flots contained identifiable remains and they have been listed in Table 4.4. Six of the 15 late Iron Age to Roman flots contained identifiable remains and they have been listed in Table 4.5.

Some of the flots also contained numerous mollusc shells. In the case of the 5000 series of sample numbers, they were mostly of the small burrowing species

Table 4.1 Waterlogged macroscopic plant remains from the late Iron Age well 29/9 (seeds unless otherwise stated)

			No. of items	
	Sample		29/6	29/5
	Context		29/25	29/24
	Weight processed (kg)		1	1
Bryophyta	Moss	Leafy stems	+	-
Ranunculus cf. *acris* L.	Buttercup		-	1
R cf. *repens* L.	Buttercup		1	1
R. S. *Batrachium* sp.	Water crowfoot		28	52
Papaver rhoeas tp.	Poppy		1	5
P. somniferum L.	Opium poppy		-	1
Brassica rapa L. ssp. *sylvestris* (L.) Jan.	Wild turnip		1	-
Thlaspi arvense L.	Field penny-cress		-	1
Capsella bursa-pastoris (L.) Medic.	Shepherd's purse		2	4
Cruciferae indet.			4	2
Cerastium cf. *fontanum* Baum.	Mouse-ear chickweed		6	6
Stellaria media gp.	Chickweed		31	60
Arenaria sp.	Sandwort		11	-
Chenopodium polyspermum L.	All-seed		21	12
C. album L.	Fat hen		2	4
C. rubrum gp.	Red goosefoot		-	1
Atriplex sp.	Orache		1	3
Malva sylvestris L.	Common mallow		3	11
Potentilla anserina L.	Silverweed		1	-
P. reptans L.	Creeping cinquefoil		-	1
Agrimonia eupatoria L.	Agrimony		-	1
Prunus or *Crataegus* tp.	Sloe or hawthorn	Thorn	2	-
Epilobium sp.	Willow herb		12	-
Callitriche sp.	Starwort		-	1
Aethusa cynapium L.	Fool's parsley		5	17
Pastinaca sativa L.	Wild parsnip		2	-
Torilis sp.	Hedge-parsley		5	8
Daucus carota L.	Wild carrot		-	1
Polygonum aviculare agg.	Knotgrass		11	7
P. persicaria L.	Red shank		20	2
Rumex crispus L.	Curled dock		1	1
R. conglomeratus Mur.	Sharp dock		142	709
Rumex sp.	Dock		120	16
Rumex sp.	Dock	Stem with pedicules	6	27
Urtica urens L.	Small nettle		3	1
U. dioica L.	Stinging nettle		643	1021
Myosotis sp.	Forget-me-not		-	1
Hyoscyamus niger L.	Henbane		5	1
Ballota nigra L.	Black horehound		12	-
Lamium sp. (not *album*)	Dead-nettle		1	-
Galeopsis tetrahit agg.	Hemp-nettle		1	1
Plantago major L.	Great plantain		143	71
Valerianella locusta (L.) Lat.	Lamb's lettuce		-	1
Tripleurospermum inodorum (L.) Sch.	Scentless mayweed		-	1
Arctium sp.	Burdock		2	-
Carduus sp.	Thistle		17	1
cf. Cirsium sp.	Thistle		13	9
Leontodon sp.	Hawkbit		-	1
Sonchus asper (L.) Hill	Sow-thistle		19	56
Crepis capillaris (L.) Wal.	Smooth hawk's-beard		1	-
Taraxacum sp.	Dandelion		2	1
Juncus bufonius gp.	Toad rush		50	10
Juncus sp.	Rush		20	20
Lemna sp.	Duckweed		8	20
Bromus sp.	Brome		2	-
Gramineae indet.	Grass		31	20
Total seeds			1,412	2,191

Table 4.2 Charred plant material from the late Iron Age well 29/9

			No. of items	
		Sample	29/6	29/5
		Context	29/25	29/24
Quercus sp.	Charcoal	Oak	+	-
Alnus / Corylus sp.	Charcoal	Alder / hazel	+	-
Bromus sp.	Seed	Brome	+	-
Triticum spelta L.	Glume base	Spelt wheat	2	1
Hordeum sp.	Grain	Barley	1	-
Cereal indet.			1	-
Hordeum sp.	Rachis	Barley	1	-
Galium aparine L.		Goosegrass	-	1
Eleocharis S. *Palustres* sp.		Spike-rush	-	1

Cecilioides acicula, along with a few examples of the dry ground open country species *Vallonia excentrica*. However, the flots from the late Iron Age waterhole 29/9 and the 3000 series from the Roman ditches contained many shells of a range of aquatic and terrestrial species likely to have lived in the features. These have been recorded in Table 4.3 on a scale of relative abundance.

Interpretation

The Iron Age

The molluscs from the late Iron Age well 29/9 included stagnant water species such as *Lymnaea truncatula* and *Anisus leucostoma*. The waterlogged seeds from Samples 29/5 and 29/6 suggested rather pond-like conditions with *Ranunculus* S. *Batrachium* sp. (water crowfoot) growing in the water and *Lemna* sp. (duckweed) growing on the surface. The insect remains included the aquatic larvae of midges (Chironomidae) and small water beetles such as *Helophorus brevipalpis* tp.

The terrestrial plant and insect remains from the well suggested open conditions, the only evidence for trees or scrub being a couple of thorns of *Prunus* or *Crataegus* sp. (sloe or hawthorn). The plant remains very much represented a flora of dry ground with, for example, seeds of Cyperaceae (sedges) absent and, in comparison with Iron Age sites on the lower terraces or floodplain, low numbers of seeds of *Juncus* spp. (rushes). Numerous seeds of *Plantago major* (great plantain) suggested an area of trampled ground in the vicinity of the well. Otherwise, the major category of vegetation on the site suggested weedy neglected or waste ground with *Rumex conglomeratus* (sharp dock) and *Urtica dioica* (stinging nettle). There were somewhat smaller numbers of seeds from annual weeds of more frequently disturbed and perhaps rather nutrient-rich ground, such as *Stellaria media* gp. (chickweed), *Chenopodium polyspermum* (all-seed) and *Sonchus asper* (sow-thistle). Some of these seeds could have been introduced amongst crops brought to the site for processing, although the undoubted arable weed seeds from the charred flots (see below) were mostly from other species. There were no waterlogged remains of definite crops from the well although *Papaver somniferum* (opium poppy) could have been cultivated. The two well samples contained a few charred remains of *Triticum spelta* (spelt wheat) and *Hordeum* sp. (barley). There were very few waterlogged seeds of grassland plants. The terrestrial insects likewise largely comprised a fauna of weedy disturbed ground and there were few dung beetles. Unlike some of the Iron Age sites on the floodplain, where scarabaeid dung beetles comprise around 20% of the terrestrial Coleoptera, numbers of these beetles were relatively low. There were, however, some beetles which feed on the roots of grassland plants such as *Phyllopertha horticola* and *Agriotes* sp.

The early and middle Iron Age charred plant remains (excluding charcoal) appeared to have been almost entirely derived from crop processing. The assemblages can be divided into two groups. Samples 5001 to 5013 generally contained high concentrations of weed seeds and some also had high concentrations of cereal grain. Quantities of chaff were much lower. Samples 5014 to 5030 mostly had lower concentrations of remains. The only crops identified with certainty were *Triticum spelta* (spelt wheat) and *Hordeum vulgare* (six-row hulled barley). It is possible that a little *T. dicoccum* was also present but the few grains of *Avena* sp. probably represented wild oat. Although grains of wheat outnumbered grains of barley, barley was present in more samples than wheat. The chaff was almost entirely glumes from hulled wheat, probably spelt, with only a single rachis fragment of barley. The weed seeds were mostly from arable weeds of well-drained circumneutral soils as might be expected on the Second Gravel Terrace upon which the site is situated, for example *Atriplex* sp. (orache), *Medicago lupulina* (black medick) and *Lithospermum arvense* (corn gromwell). Nitrophilous weeds were not much in evidence and some of the samples had a significant proportion of Leguminosae seeds, possibly reflecting relatively low levels of soil fertility. The occurrence of *Galium aparine* (goosegrass) seeds in almost half the samples was possibly indicative of autumn sowing of some of the cereals. Seeds of some wayside plants such as Malvaceae (mallow) had become incorporated into one of the assemblages, perhaps as a result of arable extending onto areas that were previously uncultivated. Seeds of marsh plants, particularly *Eleocharis* S. *Palustres* sp. (spike rush), were abundant in some but by no means all of the flots.

Table 4.3 Molluscs

	Late Iron Age well 29/9						Roman ditches								
Sample	29/6	29/5	29/4	29/3	29/2	29/1	3001	3003	3004	3006	3007	3008	3009	3010	3011
Context	29/25	29/24	29/23	29/22	29/12	29/10	3446	3263	3266	3303	3329	3483	3383	3376	3413
Valvata cristata (Müll.)	-	-	-	-	-	-	-	+	-	+	+	+	-	-	-
Carychium sp.	2	-	-	-	+	++	-	+	+	+	+	+	++	-	+
Aplexa hypnorum (L.)	3	-	+	+	+	-	-	-	-	-	-	-	-	-	-
Lymnaea truncatula (Müll.)	2	7	-	+	+	+	-	+	+	-	-	-	+	-	+
Planorbis planorbis (L.)	-	-	-	-	-	-	+	+	+	+	-	+	-	-	-
Anisus leucostoma (Mil.)	3	4	+	+	+	+	++	-	+	+++	+	+++	+	-	-
Armiger crista (L.)	-	-	-	-	-	-	-	+++	++	+	-	-	-	-	-
Succinea or *Oxyloma* sp.	-	1	-	-	-	-	-	-	-	+	-	-	-	-	-
Cochlicopa sp.	-	-	-	-	+	++	-	+	+	+	-	+	-	-	+
Vertigo antivertigo (Drap.)	-	-	-	-	-	-	-	-	+	+	-	+	+	-	+
V. pygmaea (Drap.)	-	-	-	-	-	+	+	+	+	+	-	-	-	-	+
V. angustior (Jeff.)	-	-	-	-	-	-	-	-	-	-	-	-	-	-	+
Pupilla muscorum (L.)	1	2	-	-	+	+	-	+	-	+	+	+	+	-	+
Vallonia costata (Müll.)	2	1	+	+	-	+++	+	+	+	-	+	-	-	-	-
V. excentrica Sterk.	1	2	-	++	-	+++	++	++	++	+	+	+	-	-	+++
Acanthinula aculeata (Müll.)	-	-	-	-	-	-	-	-	-	-	-	-	-	-	-
Punctum pygmaeum (Drap.)	1	-	-	-	+	+	-	-	-	-	+	-	-	-	+
Discus rotundatus (Müll.)	-	-	-	-	-	-	+	-	-	-	-	-	+	-	+
Nesovitrea hammonis (Ström)	-	-	-	-	-	-	-	+	-	-	-	-	+	-	+
Aegopinella nitidula (Drap.)	-	-	-	-	-	-	-	-	-	-	-	-	-	-	-
Oxychilus cellarius (Ström)	-	-	+	+	+	+	-	-	-	-	-	-	-	-	-
Clausilia bidentata (Ström)	-	-	-	-	-	-	-	-	-	-	-	-	-	-	-
Trichia hispida gp.	6	12	+	++	++	+++	+	+++	++	++	++	+	+	+	++
Total	21	29													

+ scarce, ++ moderately common, +++ abundant

Table 4.4a Early and middle Iron Age charred plant remains

		Total number of items									
	Sample	29/7	5000	5001	5002	5003	5004	5005	5006	5008	5009
	Context	29/75	5312	5503	5503	5470	5509	5321	5476	5702	5746
	Sample Volume (l)	2	12	14	15	12	6	4	6	21	8
	Date	MIA	EIA	MIA	MIA	MIA	MIA	MIA	MIA	MIA	MIA
Cereal Grain											
Triticum spelta L.	Spelt wheat	-	-	-	-	1	-	-	-	3	19
Triticum sp.	Wheat	-	1	1	-	4	-	-	-	11	43
Triticum cf. *dicoccum* Shübl.	Emmer	-	-	-	-	-	-	-	-	1	-
Hordeum sp.	Hulled barley	-	1	-	2	1	4	-	-	3	2
Hordeum vulgare L.	6-row hulled barley	-	-	-	-	1	-	-	-	-	1
Hordeum sp.	Barley	1	-	-	-	-	1	2	2	8	2
Avena sp.	Oats	-	-	-	-	1	-	-	-	-	-
cf *Avena* sp.	Oats	-	-	-	-	1	-	-	-	-	-
Cereal indet.		-	2	1	1	32	7	6	1	64	121
Total Cereal Grain		1	4	2	3	41	12	8	3	90	188
Cereal Chaff											
Triticum spelta L. glume	Spelt wheat	-	-	-	-	2	3	-	4	4	8
T. dicoccum Shübl. or *spelta* L. glume	Emmer or spelt wheat	-	-	-	-	2	10	-	6	12	26
Hordeum sp. rachis	Barley	-	-	-	-	-	-	-	-	-	1
Avena sp. awn	Oats	-	-	-	-	-	-	-	1	1	-
Total Chaff (excluding awns)		-	-	-	-	4	13	-	10	16	35
Seeds of Other Crop or Collected Plants											
Corylus avellana L.	Hazel	-	1	-	-	-	-	-	-	-	-
Weed Seeds											
Ranunculus. cf. *repens* L.	Buttercup	-	-	-	-	-	-	-	-	1	-
Papaver rhoeas tp.	Poppy	-	-	-	1	-	-	-	-	-	-
P. argemone L.	Poppy	-	-	2	2	-	-	-	-	-	-
Fumaria sp.	Fumitory	-	-	-	-	-	-	-	-	-	1
Brassica rapa L. ssp. *sylvestris* (L.) Jan.	Wild turnip	-	-	-	-	-	-	-	-	-	1
Stellaria media gp.	Chickweed	-	-	-	-	1	2	-	-	2	5
Montia fontana L. ssp. *chondrosperma* (Fenz.) Walt.	Blinks	-	-	-	-	-	-	-	-	3	-
Chenopodium album L.	Fat hen	-	-	-	-	1	2	-	-	3	4
Chenopodiaceae indet.		-	3	2	3	2	2	-	1	6	6
Atriplex sp.	Orache	-	-	2	3	-	-	-	-	1	26
Malva sylvestris L.	Common mallow	-	-	1	-	-	-	-	-	-	-
Malvaceae indet.	Mallow	-	-	22	22	-	-	-	-	-	1
Vicia or *Lathyrus* sp.	Vetch or tare	-	-	1	1	1	-	-	-	7	1
Medicago lupulina L.	Black medick	-	-	2	3	-	-	-	-	-	-
cf. *Medicago lupulina* L.	Black medick	-	-	5	7	3	-	1	1	1	2
Trifolium sp.	Clovers, trefoils	-	-	-	-	-	-	-	-	1	1
Aphanes arvensis L.	Parsley-piert	-	-	1	1	-	-	-	-	-	-
Euphorbia sp.	Spurge	-	-	-	-	-	-	-	-	-	1
Polygonum aviculare agg.	Knotgrass	-	-	-	-	-	1	-	1	1	6
Fallopia convolvulus (L.) Löve	Black bindweed	-	-	2	-	1	2	-	-	3	2
Rumex acetosella agg.	Sheep's sorrel	-	-	1	-	-	-	-	-	-	-
Rumex sp.	Dock	-	3	1	1	1	2	-	-	3	4
Urtica dioica L.	Stinging nettle	-	-	-		1	-	-	-	-	-
Cf. Anagallis arvensis L.	Scarlet pimpernel	-	-	7	8	-	-	-	-	-	-
Lithospermum arvense L.	Corn gromwell	-	-	12	16	-	1	-	-	12	4
Hyoscyamus niger L.	Henbane	-	-	-	-	1	1	-	-	-	1
Odontites verna (Bell.) Dum.	Red bartsia	-	-	10	5	-	1	-	-	1	-
Plantago lanceolata L.	Ribwort plantain	-	-	1	-	2	-	-	-	1	-
Sherardia arvensis L.	Field madder	-	-	-	1	-	-	-	-	2	-
Galium aparine L.	Goosegrass	-	-	7	7	1	1	-	2	2	2
Tripleurospermum inodorum (L.) Sch.	Scentless mayweed	-	1	4	6	-	1	-	-	1	2
Arctium sp.	Burdock	-	-	-	-	1	-	-	-	-	-
Carduus or *Cirsium* sp.	Thistle	-	-	-	-	-	-	-	-	1	1
Juncus effusus gp.	Rush	-	-	-	-	-	59	-	-	-	-
Eleocharis S. *Palustres* sp.	Spike rush	-	-	-	-	5	2	-	1	14	1
Carex spp.	Sedges	-	-	-	-	-	4	-	-	-	2
Gramineae indet.	Grasses	-	1	2	1	3	1	1	3	3	3
Bromus cf. *secalinus* L.	Brome	-	-	-	-	-	-	1	-	1	2
Weed indet.		-	3	48	25	31	15	-	8	39	21
Total Weed Seeds		-	11	133	113	55	97	3	17	109	100
Average number of items per litre (excluding awns)	0.5	1.3	9.6	7.7	8.3	20.3	2.8	5.0	10.2	40.4	

Table 4.4b Early and middle Iron Age charred plant remains

		Total number of items						
	Sample	5012	5014	5017	5018	5022	5023	5024
	Context	5824	5227	5553	5408	5757	5524	5589
	Sample Volume (l)	12	9	8	10	8	8	12
	Date	MIA	MIA	MIA	E or MIA	MIA	MIA	MIA
Cereal Grain								
Triticum sp.	Wheat	-	-	1	-	-	1	-
Hordeum sp.	Hulled barley	1	-	-	-	-	-	-
Hordeum sp.	Barley	5	-	-	1	1	2	5
Cereal indet.		22	3	-	1	4	-	9
Total Cereal Grain		28	3	1	2	5	3	14
Cereal Chaff								
Triticum spelta L. glume	Spelt wheat	-	-	-	1	-	-	2
T. dicoccum Shübl. or *spelta* L. glume	Emmer or spelt wheat	3	-	-	1	-	1	1
Avena sp. awn	Oats	2	-	-	-	-	-	-
Total Chaff (excluding awns)		3	-	-	2	-	1	3
Weed Seeds								
Ranunculus cf. *acris* L.	Buttercup	1	-	-	-	-	-	-
Fumaria sp.	Fumitory	3	-	-	-	-	-	-
Stellaria media gp.	Chickweed	-	-	1	-	1	-	-
Montia fontana L. ssp. *chondrosperma* (Fenz.) Walt.	Blinks	3	-	-	-	-	-	-
Chenopodium album L.	Fat hen	2	-	-	1	-	-	-
Chenopodiaceae indet.		4	-	-	1	-	-	-
Atriplex sp.	Orache	3	-	-	-	-	-	-
Malvaceae indet.	Mallow	1	-	3	-	-	-	-
Vicia or *Lathyrus* sp.	Vetch or tare	1	-	2	-	-	-	1
cf. *Medicago lupulina* L.	Black medick	-	1	-	-	-	-	2
Trifolium sp.	Clovers, trefoils	2	-	-	-	-	-	-
Polygonum aviculare agg.	Knotgrass	2	-	-	-	-	-	-
Fallopia convolvulus (L.) Löve	Black bindweed	3	-	-	1	-	-	-
Rumex sp.	Dock	1	-	-	-	-	1	1
Lithospermum arvense L.	Corn gromwell	1	-	-	-	-	-	-
Odontites verna (Bell.) Dum	Red bartsia	3	1	1	-	1	1	-
Galium aparine L.	Goosegrass	3	-	3	-	-	2	1
Tripleurospermum inodorum (L.) Sch.	Scentless mayweed	1	-	1	-	-	-	-
Eleocharis S. Palustres sp.	Spike rush	4	-	-	1	-	-	1
Carex spp.	Sedges	2	-	-	-	-	-	-
Gramineae indet.	Grasses	-	-	2	-	-	1	1
Bromus cf. *secalinus* L.	Brome	-	-	-	-	1	-	-
Weed indet.		15	1	15	-	1	1	4
Total Weed Seeds		55	3	28	4	4	6	11
Total no of items per litre excluding awns		7.2	0.7	3.6	0.8	1.1	1.3	2.3

This suggested that some of the crops being processed on the site were from fields which extended onto the clay slope at the edge of the Second Terrace or were situated on lower lying ground towards the river.

The results from the Iron Age site generally present a similar picture to those from the Ashville Trading Estate (Jones 1978). The Ashville results likewise showed spelt wheat and six-row hulled barley to be the two main crops. There was also evidence from the weed seeds for cultivation extending into wetter, lower lying ground.

The Roman period

The molluscs from the 5000 series of samples, both Iron Age and Roman, reflected the dry, open and somewhat disturbed conditions of the site on the Second Gravel Terrace. Apart from recent burrowing species, the fauna comprised mostly *Vallonia excentrica*, with a few *V. costata*, *Pupilla muscorum* and *Trichia hispida* gp. The flots from the Roman ditches on the lower edge of the terrace, however, contained much richer molluscan assemblages with strong wet ground and aquatic elements. These flots contained the same dry ground species which had probably fallen into the ditches. There were also large numbers of *Anisus leucostoma*, a stagnant water species which can tolerate the drying out of its habitat. The occurrence of *Valvata cristata* and *Armiger crista* suggests that water flowed along the ditches for some of the year and that they were well vegetated with water weed. The marsh species from these flots included *Vertigo angustior*, a species now very rare in Britain. It had probably been able to extend up the Roman ditches from a more extensive marsh habitat on the Gault Clay or the floodplain.

The charred plant remains from the late Iron Age and Roman flots were similar to those from the early and middle Iron Age samples, although the concentration of remains was lower. Spelt wheat and barley were again the only certain crops.

Table 4.4c Early and middle Iron Age charred plant remains

		Total number of items							
	Sample	5026	5030	5032	5036	5037	5048	5049	5050
	Context	5791	5901	5231	5922	5009	5886	5310	6247
	Sample Volume (l)	12	8	11	15	14	6	4	12
	Date	MIA	E/MIA	MIA	E/MIA	MIA	MIA	MIA	MIA
Cereal Grain									
Triticum spelta L.	Spelt wheat	-	-	2	-	-	-	-	-
Triticum sp.	Wheat	1	-	2	-	1	1	-	-
Hordeum sp.	Hulled barley	-	-	-	-	1	-	-	-
Hordeum sp.	Barley	1	-	-	-	-	-	-	-
Cereal indet.		5	6	13	8	12	4	2	3
Total Cereal Grain		7	6	17	8	14	5	2	3
Cereal Chaff									
Triticum dicoccum Shübl. or *spelta* L. glume	Emmer or spelt wheat	-	-	4	-	1	4	4	4
Hordeum sp. rachis	Barley	-	-	-	-	-	-	1	-
Avena sp. awn	Oats	-	-	1	-	1	-	-	1
Total Chaff (excluding awns)		-	-	4	-	1	4	5	4
Weed Seeds									
Stellaria media gp.	Chickweed	1	-	-	-	-	-	-	-
Montia fontana L. ssp. *chondrosperma* (Fenz.) Walt.	Blinks	-	-	-	1	1	-	-	-
Malvaceae indet.	Mallow	-	1	-	-	-	-	-	-
Vicia or *Lathyrus* sp.	Vetch or tare	3	-	-	4	-	1	2	4
cf. *Medicago lupulina* L.	Black medick	-	-	-	-	4	1	-	-
Trifolium sp.	Clovers, trefoils	-	-	-	-	1	-	-	-
Potentilla sp.		-	-	1	-	-	-	-	-
Polygonum persicaria L.	Redshank	1	-	-	-	-	-	-	-
Rumex sp.	Dock	-	-	1	-	-	4	-	-
Urtica dioica L.	Stinging nettle	-	-	1	-	-	-	-	-
Hyoscyamus niger L.	Henbane	-	-	1	-	-	-	-	-
Odontites verna (Bell.) Dun.	Red bartsia	-	-	2	-	-	1	-	-
Galium aparine L.	Goosegrass	-	-	-	-	-	2	-	-
Tripleurospermum inodorum (L.) Sch.	Scentless mayweed	-	-	-	1	-	-	-	-
Eleocharis S. *Palustres* sp.	Spike rush	1	-	1	-	1	2	-	2
Carex spp.	Sedges	-	-	-	-	-	3	-	-
Gramineae indet.	Grasses	1	-	3	1	-	-	-	-
Bromus cf. *secalinus* L.	Brome	-	-	1	-	-	-	-	1
Weed indet.		-	-	10	7	2	4	-	1
Total Weed Seeds		7	1	21	14	9	18	2	8
Total no of items per litre (excluding awns)		1.2	0.9	3.8	1.5	1.7	4.5	2.3	1.3

Table 4.5 Late Iron Age and Roman charred plant remains

		Total number of items					
	Sample	3003	3004	5031	5044	5045	5047
	Context	3263	3266	5179	6211	6233	5354
	Sample Volume (l)	7	9	14	12	10	12
	Date	C2nd AD	C2nd AD	LIA	C1st – 2nd AD	C1st – 2nd AD	C1st – 2nd AD
Cereal Grain							
Triticum spelta L.	Spelt wheat	-	-	-	-	-	1
Triticum sp.	Wheat	-	1	1	-	-	1
Hordeum sp.	Barley	-	-	-	3	2	3
Cereal indet.		-	1	9	-	5	5
Total Cereal Grain		-	2	10	3	7	10
Cereal Chaff							
Triticum spelta L. glume	Spelt wheat	-	-	3	1	-	-
T. dicoccum Shübl. or *spelta* L. glume	Emmer or spelt wheat	-	-	6	-	5	7
Hordeum sp. rachis	Barley	-	-	-	-	-	1
Total Chaff		-	-	9	1	5	8
Weed Seeds							
Ranunculus cf. *repens* L.	Buttercup	-	-	-	-	-	1
Stellaria media gp.	Chickweed	-	-	-	-	-	1
Malvaceae indet.	Mallow	-	-	-	-	1	1
Vicia or *Lathyrus* sp.	Vetch or tare	-	-	-	-	-	5
cf. *Medicago lupulina* L.	Black medick	-	-	-	-	1	2
Fallopia convolvulus (L.) Löve	Black bindweed	1	-	-	-	-	-
Rumex sp.	Dock	-	-	-	-	1	-
Lithospermum arvense L.	Corn gromwell	-	-	1	-	-	-
Odontites verna (Bell.) Dum.	Red bartsia	-	-	-	-	-	1
Galium aparine L.	Goosegrass	-	-	3	-	-	-
Eleocharis S. *Palustres* sp.	Spike rush	-	-	1	-	-	-
Carex spp.	Sedges	-	-	-	-	-	1
Weed indet.		-	1	5	-	5	5
Total Weed Seeds		1	1	10	-	8	17
Average no of items per litre		0.1	0.3	2.1	0.3	2.0	2.9

Table 4.6 Fragment frequency and percentage of animal bones according to period

	Trench 29		Trench 32		Trench 33							
	M-LIA		Roman		Earlier IA		MIA		All IA		Roman	
Species	No.	%	No.	%	No.	%	No.	%	No.	%	No.	%
Cattle	25	39	5	38	52	36	284[4]	37	336	37	89[6]	41
Sheep/goat[1]	23	35	1	8	67	47	349	46	416	46	74	34
Pig[2]	8	12	-	-	14	10	49	6	63	7	16	7
Horse	9	13	7	54	6[3]	4	61[5]	8	67	7	32	15
Dog	-	-	-	-	3	2	17	2	20	2	5	2
Red deer	A	-	-	-	-	-	-	-	-	-	-	-
Mouse (*Apodemus* sp.)	-	-	-	-	1	1	-	-	1	-	-	-
Identified bones	65+A		13		143		760		903		216	
Unidentified	120		79		210		837		1047		211	
Total	185+A		92		353		1597		1950		427	
Burnt	1		-		3		30		33		-	
Bird	-		-		-		-		-		7[7]	

Notes A = Antler fragment
1 = Includes goat tooth and horn core
2 = Includes possible wild pig ulna
3 = Includes horse cranium
4 = Includes two cattle crania but excludes 16 bones of cattle forelimb and 22 cattle vertebrae
5 = Includes two horse mandibles
6 = Includes a cattle cranium
7 = Includes six bones of raven and one of duck cf. mallard. Also two frog bones

THE ANIMAL BONE *by Bob Wilson with Alison Locker identifying the bird bones*

Introduction

The main interest in examining the animal bones from Wyndyke Furlong was to look at the similarities between them and the original assemblage excavated at Ashville.

Numbers of bone fragments

From the three new excavation trenches yielding animal bones, over 2673 ordinarily collected bones and 619 sieved bones were examined and put into an archaeological context of one kind or another. Table 4.6 shows information on the species recorded. Dated sheep/goat bones may include goat as two such elements were identified among the unphased bones. The latter group also yielded a large pig ulna which might be of wild pig. With the exception of raven and possible wild pig, the species represented are identical to those recorded previously at Ashville.

In Table 4.6 the species and other categories of bones tend to be of small sample size so bones from early and early-middle Iron Age phase groups have been added together to increase the size of the early Iron Age group for comparison. Percentages of Iron Age species bones in Trench 33 are more similar to each other than to the Roman group, although percentages of the latter resemble those from the small group of middle to late Iron Age bones from Trench 29. In general percentages of sheep are lower and those of cattle are higher than those recorded previously at Ashville (Wilson *et al.*1978, table XIV).

At Ashville species percentages were found to differ according to the type of feature they were recovered from, namely pits and ditches, the former tending to yield greater quantities of the medium sized species, ie sheep and pig. This is a pattern found elsewhere and is often related to how bones of different sizes are distributed in space over sites (Wilson 1996, 70–73). Table 4.7 shows the separation of bones according to feature type amongst the middle Iron Age assemblage, the largest of the chronological groups in Table 4.6. There are small percentage differences of sheep and pig among groups but the combined percentages of the two species retain the expected pattern between feature types, especially between pits and linear ditches.

Table 4.7 also shows percentages of species and other bones according to a small sample of identified bones amongst the sieved bones. The representation of sheep, and sheep and pig bones collectively, are greater than those in the middle Iron Age feature type groups, and similar findings of sieved samples elsewhere show that small and medium sized species are better represented (Wilson 1978; Wilson and Allison 1990, 59). Burnt and unidentified bones are also better represented in sieved samples. These findings, of course, show the better retrieval of small bones and fragments in sieved samples compared to handpicked groups.

Table 4.8 takes the analysis one stage further by comparing the skeletal element representation among the sheep/goat bones in the pit and linear ditch groups of middle Iron Age bones, the only groups large enough to allow a moderately reliable comparison of species elements. Percentages of head, foot and body bones are variable but are similar to those found on other regional Iron Age sites. The index of bone degradation (Wilson

Table 4.7 Fragment frequency and percentage of handpicked bones according to type of middle Iron Age feature in Trench 33 and according to soil sieving

Feature type	Ring ditches		Linear ditches		Gullies		Pits		Wells		Post holes	Sieved samples	
Species	No.	%	No.	%	No.	%	No.	%	No.	%	No.	No.	%
Cattle	40	43	95	42	48	36	58[1.]	31	43[2.]	36	-	6	14
Sheep/goat	45	48	95	42	63	47	93	50	52	44	1	33	75
Pig	3	3	10	4	10	7	21	11	5	4	-	2	5
Horse	5	5	19	8	9	7	10	5	18[3.]	15	-	2	5
Dog	-	-	8	4	4	3	4	2	1	1	-	-	-
Vole (*Arvicola* sp.)	-	-	-	-	-	-	-	-	-	-	-	1	2
Identified bones	93		227		134		186		119		1	44	
Unidentified	88		289		117		236		104		3	615	
Total	181		516		251		422		223		4	619	
Burnt	1		10		2		15		2		-	131	

Notes 1 = Includes cattle cranium but excludes 22 articulated vertebrae fragments
2 = Includes cattle cranium but excludes 16 bones of cattle limb
3 = Includes 2 horse mandibles

1985) shows that bones from the site are relatively well-preserved for a prehistoric assemblage, and those from pits are better preserved than those from ditches. There is a small difference in the percentage of small bones of sheep collected, which indicates recovery or preservation of them was slightly greater in the pit group than in the ditch group.

Skeletons, articulated bone groups and crania

These are of interest in that they may indicate a deposit with symbolic or ritual significance (Grant 1984a; Hill 1995). Probably the most significant are: a dog skeleton of at least 60 bones retrieved from a once complete individual, not quite mature – an unfused proximal humerus is present – in unphased pit F5843: four wing bones and two leg bones of raven, probably from the same bird, and a cattle cranium with small horncores of a mature beast in Roman ditch F5703 (part of 5359); some 22 fragmented vertebrae of a cattlebeast in middle Iron Age pit F5553: a cattle cranium with horn cores broken off and 16 bones of a right forelimb, humerus to third phalanges in middle Iron Age well F5664; a cattle cranium with horn cores broken off in middle Iron Age pit F5369; a horse cranium of an animal aged about 4½ years in early Iron Age pit F5960; a mandible or horse about two years of age in middle Iron Age well F5664; a mandible of horse older than 4-5 years of age in middle Iron Age ditch F5624; two mandibles of different horses, one aged 2½-5 years in middle Iron Age ditch F5686; two horse mandibles, both incomplete in middle Iron Age well F5664.

It is possible that crania and mandibles of other animals had symbolic significance too, so the list is partial but nevertheless a start in the search for any potentially interesting material associations, such as those with whole pots, which may have been deposited at the same time as the bones. The pit deposits may be comparable to the 'special deposits' at Danebury (Grant 1984a) and the well deposits seem comparable to a cattle cranium in a Bronze Age well near Radley (Hamilton-Dyer 1995) and a dog cranium in an Iron Age well at Thrupp (Wilson 1997).

Information on age at death of animals

Table 4.9 records the mandible wear stages of the three main species. Only the middle Iron Age group of sheep mandible stages is large enough to compare with those of other sites. It is generally similar to other Iron Age and Roman sample distributions although it has a smaller proportion of MWSs of lambs than the previous

Table 4.8 Grouped skeletal elements of sheep/goat bones from pits and ditches

	Pits	Linear ditches
Sample size	93	95
	%	%
Head	17	35
Feet	24	9
Body	59	56
Degradation index	39	57
Small bones	2	-

Table 4.9 Mandible wear stages at death

Species	EIA	MIA	Roman
Cattle		39, 42	19, 41, 43e
Sheep	4e, 31, 37, 38e	5e, 9, 9e, 10e, 11e, 11e, 21, 22, 22e, 22e, 23, 29, 30, 31e, 32, 32e, 33, 38, 39, 40, 41, 41e, 43, 44	30, 39, 40e
Pig	33e	21, 36e	10e, 28

Note e = estimated MWS (Grant 1982)

Ashville sample (Hamilton 1978). A sizeable group of fragmentary lamb mandibles had lost diagnostic teeth and their MWSs could not be completed to add to those of better preserved mandibles.

In the previous Ashville assemblage all the Iron Age horse bones appeared to be from mature individuals (Wilson 1978, fig. 71) but here one epiphysis in each of the Iron Age and Roman samples (n = 14 and 15 respectively) is from an immature individual. Moreover, horse crania or mandibles were from a two year old individual, a two to five year old, another aged about 4½ years, while another was from an older skeletally mature horse.

Bone measurements

Table 4.10 presents a selection of measurements from the more or less complete bones that were found. There are too few measurements to analyse the results here, except to say they are similar in size to measurements of Iron Age and Roman bones elsewhere (Wilson 1978, tables XIX, XX and XXI).

Pathology

Slight periosteosis was found on one middle Iron Age sheep mandible, MWS 28-36 (F5779) and on one Roman sheep mandible, MWS 24-30 (F5007). The lateral joints of two Roman lumbar vertebrae of horse (F5703 part of 5359) were fused. A Roman dog radius and ulna were fused together with no sign of fractures (F5359).

Table 4.10 Bone measurements: greatest length of elements (GL) in mm.

Species	Bone element	Iron Age	Romano-British
Cattle	Radius	246, 266, 281	
	Metacarpal	187	169e, 177
	Metatarsal	201, 203	
Sheep	Humerus	128, 128	
	Metacarpal	116	
	Metatarsal	114, 122	
Horse	Radius		199e
	Tibia		303
	Metacarpal		225e
	Metatarsal	243	
Dog	Tibia	179	

Chapter 5: Discussion and Conclusions

by Jeff Muir

INTRODUCTION

The Iron Age settlement at Wyndyke Furlong was located in a landscape rich in natural resources. Then as now, the gravel terraces of the Upper Thames Valley provided a near ideal growing environment for arable crops which was extensively exploited by Iron Age and Roman farmers. Environmental evidence recovered during the original Ashville excavations proved that the settlement inhabitants were engaged in intensive cereal production and that it formed the basis of their economy. Far from challenging those original conclusions, the evidence from Wyndyke Furlong provides broad confirmation of the nature of the settlement.

The archaeology of the site falls into four broad phases. The earliest prehistoric phase was represented entirely by artefactual evidence consisting of worked flint and a small amount of pottery including beaker. No negative features could be certainly attributed to this phase and the majority of finds were redeposited in later features. During the Iron Age a small village or hamlet was established which was characterised by circular buildings, enclosure ditches and pits. Towards the end of the middle Iron Age there was a major settlement re-organisation when the village was abandoned or relocated and the land presumably turned over to cultivation. A track or droveway became the focal point of a new, Romano-British field system which was defined by deep drainage ditches. This field system was itself overlain at a later date by a new network of medieval fields and ditches whose axis appeared to partially reflect the Roman arrangement.

EARLIER PREHISTORIC ACTIVITY

The earlier prehistoric evidence consisted almost entirely of redeposited artefacts recovered from Iron Age contexts. A simple plot of the worked flint and Bronze Age pottery revealed overlapping distributions which were broadly concentrated at the western end of Trench 33. Although based on a relatively small number of artefacts the spatial distribution was sufficiently well defined to suggest a genuine focus of earlier prehistoric activity (Fig. 2.8). The location of the artefact distribution to the south west of ditch 6304 may add credence to the suggestion that the ditch was of pre-Iron Age origin.

During the original Ashville excavations a pair of Bronze Age ring ditches and associated cremations were excavated (Balkwill 1978, 25–30). Environmental evidence recovered from the cremation deposits suggested that food was deliberately placed in the funeral pyre as part of an offering to the dead. Although Balkwill argues that the food may have been transported to the ring ditches from elsewhere, local cultivation was not disproved and it is possible that the artefactual evidence found at Wyndyke Furlong is the remnant of low level Bronze Age domestic activity.

Evidence of Bronze Age settlement is becoming increasingly well documented in the region. At Eight Acre Field, Radley, evidence of a middle to late Bronze Age double-ditched enclosure was revealed along with field boundaries and waterholes (Mudd 1995). At Corporation Farm to the south of Abingdon, a series of enclosures and a roundhouse structure lay at the centre of a presumed mixed farming settlement (Shand 1985). Such settlement evidence combined with the impressive density of Bronze Age funerary monuments in the area confirms that the landscape was well ordered and fully utilised during this period.

THE IRON AGE

The early settlement

The full extent of early Iron Age activity at Wyndyke Furlong is difficult to clearly define. This is partly due to problems caused by redeposition of pottery sherds, and partly, it is suspected, because a high proportion of early Iron Age structures may have been post-built. The problem of recognising such structures was aggravated by the density of the posthole clusters and by the relatively small proportion of postholes which were excavated. Less than half of the excavated postholes contained any dating evidence.

Post-built structures

A total of five post-built structures were tentatively identified as belonging to the early or early-middle Iron Age (5087 and 5257; 5166 and 6310; and 6313). As their post rings overlapped, it was clear that not all of these structures were contemporary. Structures 5087 and 5257 were thought to be the earlier of the four, based on analysis of the limited pottery. Both structures were approximately circular, each with a 6 m wide gap in the eastern side. Such a wide entrance is unusual for a roundhouse and the structures need not have been intended for human habitation. A wide doorway would have provided practical access to an animal byre or storage shed.

Circular post-built structures are a relatively common feature of the earlier to middle Iron Age (Allen *et al* 1984, 100; Cunliffe 1991, 242–44). The diameter and relative completeness of the post circles does vary considerably, however, and in many cases poor survival of the Iron Age ground surface has lead to uncertainty over whether the ring of posts represents the outer wall of a structure or an internal ring of roof supports (Allen *et al.* 1984, 91). It has been clearly demonstrated that so long as internal supports exist, the outer walls of the structure need not have been substantially constructed (Guilbert 1981, 299–317). Even so, it would seem that the doorway represented a weak point in any circular structure and as such required extra support from a pair of more substantial posts. At Wyndyke Furlong no trace of an outer wall - either in the form of stake rings or projecting door posts – survived on any of the post-built structures. In addition, the recut and generally more substantial nature of the paired 'door' postholes identified in structures 5087 and 6310 would suggest that the posthole rings marked the location of the outer walls of the circular structures.

The identification of the post-built structures is interesting, particularly given the apparent lack of such early structures at Ashville. The posthole cluster in the south-east corner of the 1974 excavations can be interpreted in more than one way, however (Parrington 1978, fig. 12). The majority of the postholes were undated and at least three appear to have been cut by Period 2 gullies, raising the possibility that post-built structures may have existed adjacent to, and have been contemporary with, the Period 1 pits.

The developed settlement

The roundhouses

Towards the middle Iron Age, construction techniques appear to have altered and the old post ring structures were replaced by ditched circular structures. Structures 6286 and 6287 appear to be two of the earliest of this type of building. The ceramic sequence in both structures points to an initial construction date between the early and middle Iron Age.

The middle Iron Age archaeology was dominated by a series of penannular and annular ditches and ring gullies which it is assumed marked the sites of roundhouses (Fig. 2.13). There were five clear examples of roundhouse structures (5021, 6282, 6283, 6286 and 6287) and another three possible examples which fell partially within the excavated area (6290, 6291 and 6297). The majority of these structures can clearly be dated to the middle Iron Age. Within that period it is equally clear that individual structures were modelled and remodelled either because of the necessity of repair or a desire to improve. Unfortunately the ceramic evidence was not sufficiently refined to be of much help in plotting that sequence of change. Similarly, the stratigraphic sequence was ill defined, the homogenous nature of feature fills often defeating careful attempts to ascertain the stratigraphic sequence.

Although long associated with Iron Age dwellings, the precise function of the penannular and annular ditches is still a matter of debate. The argument focuses on whether the gullies were used as wall slots for upright timbers or as drip gullies designed to take the runoff away from the daub walls of the roundhouse. In summarising the evidence for the Ashville structures, Parrington favoured the drip-gully theory (1978, 34).

At Wyndyke Furlong evidence from structure 5021 (Fig. 2.14) suggests that its inner gully (5340/5341) may have marked the location of the roundhouse wall rather than an external drainage gully. Although the gully was not particularly deep, it was flat bottomed and its terminals were distinctly bulbous in plan suggesting that they may have once contained upright door timbers.

Further evidence is provided by a consideration of the function of internal slots 5309 and 5343. Although both of the slots ran directly up to 5340/5341 only slot 5309 actually connected with the gully. Slot 5343 stopped immediately short of the wider gully effectively ruling out the possibility that it could have acted as an internal drainage gully carrying water to the outside of the building (Fig. 2.14). The simplest explanation is that neither of the slots were used for drainage but acted as bedding trenches for an internal division within the roundhouse. It is likely that 5309 marked the original division and was constructed at the same time as the main roundhouse wall. Slot 5343 on the other hand appears to have been dug after the main roundhouse wall was raised. Its extra length suggesting that the slot carried a new and improved internal division which replaced the old one and extended the space screened off from the rest of the roundhouse.

Structure 6286 also provided evidence for a possible-wall slot (Fig. 2.11). Gully 6139 had a stepped profile with a near vertical outside edge which would have made a good bedding trench for vertical posts. The gully was 0.50 m deep from the top of the natural gravel and, allowing for a depth of topsoil, the original depth of the gully could have been anywhere from 0.50 to 0.80 m deep. Given that the gully was cut directly into free-draining gravel, such a depth might seem unnecessary for a simple sump or drainage gully.

The gullies associated with this structure were also unusual in that they were not continuously curved but appear to have been dug in a series of straight lines. The resulting plan of the structure is reminiscent of the polygonal structures noted by Drury at Little Waltham, Essex (Drury 1978, huts C15 and C18, 23-25). There the excavator interpreted the gullies as construction trenches for post-built roundhouses. It was suggested that the polygonal shape was caused by the use of straight wall plates between the main rafters of the building (Drury 1978, 121). Polygonal gullies associated with roundhouse sites were also noted at Gravelly Guy, Stanton Harcourt in the Upper Thames Valley (Lambrick *et al.* forthcoming, enclosure Group A). The gullies were much shallower than those at little Waltham, however, and the excavator concluded that they functioned as drainage gullies.

Possible windbreak features

A number of curvilinear features (whose function remains uncertain) were noted in the northern half of Trench 33. Although semicircular gullies have been correctly interpreted as evidence for roundhouse structures in the past (eg Allen and Robinson 1993, fig. 17), in this case the arc of the gullies would appear to be too shallow to form the side of such a structure. Clusters of pits and postholes were noted adjacent to two of the structures but no clear association was established. The features have been tentatively interpreted as windbreak features, designed to protect open working areas, or the edge of the settlement from northerly winds. The best preserved of the features was structure 6072 (Fig. 2.18). The windbreak features have been very tentatively placed in the middle Iron Age on the basis of a small amount of pottery recovered from 6072. None of the other features produced dating evidence, however, and the phasing must be viewed with caution.

Pits

The spatial distribution of the pits was analysed with reference to pit clusters and to possible associations with particular ring gullies. It is clear from the plan (Fig. 2.23) that the pits were not evenly distributed across the site but concentrated in loosely defined clusters or zones. The densest pit cluster was revealed in the south-western corner of the site behind structure 5021. Although 5021 appears to have been carefully respected by all of these pits, other structures such as 6287 were not, suggesting that the pits and the circular structures could not all have been contemporary. Several of the circular structures appeared to have clusters of internal pits (6283, 6286, 6287 and 6290). In no case, however, was it possible to prove a definite stratigraphic link. Closer analysis of the pits by period did not reveal any particular concentration.

Postholes

The distribution of postholes at Wyndyke Furlong is difficult to explain. In some cases it seems fairly clear that individual groups or clusters of postholes are the remains of post-built structures. Where stratigraphic evidence exists it suggests that the posthole clusters were generally earlier than the ring gullies. In some cases it is possible that the posthole clusters may have held internal supports for roundhouse structures, but in the two clear cases where postholes fall within ring gullies (5021 and 6283), they are slightly offset and are unlikely to be contemporary. In two areas the posthole clusters are so dense that it is difficult to define any sort of structure (6314 and 6315).

Boundaries and waterholes

The north-western limit of the settlement appears to have been defined by the boundary ditch 6298 (Fig. 2.19). The ditch was relatively complex in detail, but in terms of function it appears to have divided the occupation area from what are assumed to be open fields or paddocks to the north-west. The location of waterhole 29/9 (Trench 29) would suggest that the area beyond the boundary may have been used for pasture, since cattle in particular have a high water requirement.

To the south of 6298, a narrower, more sinuous ditch (6308/6309) appeared to be associated with structures dating to the early-middle Iron Age (Fig. 2.9). It is possible that the northern end of the ditch connected with an unrecognised, earlier phase of 6298. The ditch was close to the edge of the excavation and it is unclear if there was any significant archaeology to the west of the gully.

To the north-east of the main Iron Age settlement was an isolated, rectilinear enclosure (3556) which appeared to be of the same phase (Trench 32, Fig. 2.4).The enclosure was clearly oriented on the same alignment as the later Roman track or droveway, and may have been used as an animal paddock. Given the location and alignment of the enclosure it seems reasonable to suggest that there may have been an Iron Age predecessor to the Roman trackway. Although the enclosure contained a small number of postholes, none contained artefacts and no obvious structure could be discerned from their plan. One of the postholes (3405) was truncated by the enclosure ditch 3403 suggesting that the features may have been pre-Roman in date, but without more substantial evidence it is impossible to be sure.

Settlement layout

The overall impression is of a slowly developing village or hamlet characterised by an increasingly elaborate set of structures and enclosures. It is unlikely that the features revealed at Wyndyke Furlong were at the centre of the site. The linear boundary to the north-west and the windbreak features to the north-east suggest that the area revealed was probably at northern edge of the settlement. The core would have been at Ashville or at some point between the two. It is clear that Ashville/ Wyndyke Furlong was a sizeable settlement. Up to nine roundhouses at Ashville and five or six at Wyndyke Furlong could have been standing at any one time, with the possibility of the same number again, or more, between the two excavations.

Site Economy and Status

Agriculture

The evidence of agricultural activity at Wyndyke is largely derived from the processing and analysis of plant and animal remains. The findings appear to confirm that the economy was built on a mixed agricultural regime with a particularly strong emphasis on cereal production.

The main cereal crops cultivated at both Ashville and Wyndyke Furlong were spelt wheat and six-row hulled barley. The quantity and widespread occurrence of grain recovered from features at Ashville in particular, strongly suggests that a considerable volume of cereal passed through the site. What is less certain is whether the site was a producer or a consumer of cereals. The question is an important one since much of our understanding of the site has come from the environmental analysis carried out on the cereals and associated weeds recovered. (I am grateful to Tim Allen for a useful discussion of this subject.)

It is probable, on balance, that the site was a grain producer. Although some of the flot samples were rich in grain relative to chaff, the remains appear to have been almost entirely derived from crop processing (Chapter 4). If the cereals had been fully processed elsewhere it is likely that a significantly smaller proportion of chaff and weeds would have been found. Quernstone fragments were found at both Ashville and Wyndyke Furlong suggesting that grain was ground to flour at the site.

The intensive nature of the arable regime is reflected in evidence for autumn sowing, probably of spelt wheat, and the gradual depletion of nitrogen in the soils around the site. The picture is further supported by the presence of weeds which thrive on damp and marginal lands amongst the cereal waste (Chapter 4). Ironically, the intensive nature of arable farming at the site may have contributed to its ultimate failure and abandonment.

Animal husbandry

Analysis of the faunal remains also produced a picture broadly comparable to the Ashville findings. Sheep were found to be the dominant species, although their frequency was slightly lower relative to cattle (Chapter 4). It is not unusual on middle Iron Age settlements for sheep to predominate, although it is more common in upland areas such as the Cotswolds and on the higher chalk sites of Wessex (Grant 1984b, 115–116; 1989, 136). The number of individual animals does not equate directly with the relative importance of species, however. Meat yields, for example, are obviously higher from cattle than from sheep.

Although it seems that cattle were more important at lower lying sites such as Farmoor (Wilson and Bramwell 1979, 128–133), Watkins Farm (Wilson and Allison 1990, 57–61) and Mingies Ditch (Wilson 1993, 123–134), bovine products clearly formed an important economic resource at Wyndyke Furlong. Evidence for leatherworking has already been discussed and although less archaeologically visible, meat and dairy products would undoubtedly have formed an important part of the diet. The trend towards an increased emphasis on cattle rearing in the late Iron Age and early Roman period at Wyndyke is not unusual and has been discussed elsewhere (King 1978; Grant 1989, 136–137)

Special animal deposits

The phenomenon of specially placed animal deposits on Iron Age sites in southern Britain is well known and has been much discussed (see Wilson 1992, 341–349 for discussion and Hill 1995 for an extended bibliography). Evidence for such activity at Wyndyke Furlong is limited and open to variable interpretation. A number of animal bone deposits were considered unusual enough to be noted by Wilson (Chapter 4), but in the majority of cases the bones were not associated with other 'special' deposits, nor were the contexts of deposition considered particularly meaningful (Wilson, pers. comm.). Certain deposits did hint at something more than the random deposition of domestic waste, however. Pit 5553 (Fig. 2.16), for example, contained 22 cattle vertebrae and a fragment of human skull in the same context. While the association between cattle vertebrae and human skull might be considered unusual it should be remembered that isolated pieces of human skeleton, and cranium in particular, are not particularly rare on Iron Age sites and that the association could easily be coincidental. Other deposits, such as the articulated dog skeleton in pit 5843 (Fig. 2.18) might be considered unusual enough in themselves to suggest the possibility of ritual activity, however (Wilson, pers. comm.). Interpretation of such deposits is difficult and largely a matter of subjective opinion rather than clear-cut analysis of the facts.

Domestic industry

It is clear from the artefactual evidence that although the domestic industry at Ashville could not be claimed to be of an exceptionally fine standard, it was relatively varied in scope. This led Parrington to suggest that the community was virtually self-sufficient (Parrington 1978, 37–38). The evidence from Wyndyke Furlong does not contradict this conclusion.

One of the industries represented amongst the finds assemblage was textile production. Evidence for both spinning and weaving was recovered in the form of a bone spindle whorl and fired clay loomweights. Fragments from up to nine loomweights were recovered, the majority of which came from a single pit (Chapter 3). The weights were of variable size and weight and may have been used selectively according to the type or size of the piece of work in hand. Fired or semi-baked loomweights are relatively common finds on Iron Age sites and the selection recovered from Wyndyke Furlong is comparable both in size and shape to those recovered from Gravelly Guy (Barclay and Wait, forthcoming) and Danebury (Poole 1984, 401–406).

A scrap of leather which was preserved in a small pit at Wyndyke raises the question of whether the leather was manufactured on site or was imported. However, the recovery of bone awls from both Ashville and Wyndyke Furlong suggests that even if actual tanning was not practised, leatherworking probably did take place.

Evidence for metal working at Ashville was recovered from a pair of features which were identified as smiths' working hollows (Cleere 1978, 88–90). Although iron slag was recovered from Wyndyke Furlong, the amount was small and the spatial distribution of the fragments suggests that most or all were redeposited. No focus of iron working was located and production was probably on a small scale, perhaps of purely domestic artefacts (see Chapter 3).

Trade and exchange

It is clear, both from the scale and variable nature of domestic industry, and from the range of agricultural production, that the inhabitants of Wyndyke Furlong were relatively self sufficient. Similarities in material culture and in cultural expression such as the ubiquitous triangular loomweights and ditched circular buildings which are so characteristic of the period, prove that the inhabitants could not have been completely isolated, however.

Aspects of the pottery assemblage suggest that regional trade may have taken place with communities to the north of the Thames, perhaps via the Evenlode or Cherwell valleys. In particular the presence of oolitic iron tempered wares is of interest (Chapter 3). The original source of iron ooliths in the region is the Banbury outcrop of Lower Jurassic ironstone some 40 km to the north-west of Abingdon (Doherty 1996). Although ooliths would undoubtedly have been transported down-stream through natural processes of erosion, as Doherty points out, the abundance of ooliths in the Wyndyke pottery is high enough to suggest a clay source close to the ironstone outcrop.

Although specialist potting clays were transported over some distance during the Roman period (Paul Booth pers. comm.), it is highly probable that the Wyndyke oolitic ironstone wares were manufactured close to the Banbury outcrop and so represent trade or exchange, either for the pots themselves or for their contents.

Although the community at Wyndyke clearly gained some commodities through trade, a lack of finely decorated pottery (Chapter 3) together with a complete absence of imported quernstones (Chapter 3) suggests that the site was probably of relatively low status. This may in itself be the reason for the high degree of self sufficiency, since a low status site is unlikely to be able to afford specialist goods.

Abandonment

The evidence for a major reorganisation of the landscape towards the end of the middle Iron Age is overwhelming. The settlement site itself was either abandoned or the village relocated to another site. Such change during this period was relatively common in the Upper Thames region and seems to have been a relatively widespread response to changing circumstances (Lambrick 1992, 83–84). In the case of Wyndyke Furlong, such a radical reorganisation could have come about through the growing influence of external stimuli or from a failure in the deeply rooted agricultural economy of the settlement. It is possible that both factors had a part to play.

The Ashville environmental data clearly indicates increasing nitrogen depletion of the soil and an increase in damp ground weeds amongst the processed cereal (Jones 1978, 93–110). The data can, however, be interpreted in two very different ways. The presence of damp ground weeds suggests that the area of cultivation was expanded onto the less favourable ground towards the edge or just off the gravel terrace. The reason for that expansion is the key to how we view the relative success of the Ashville/Wyndyke Furlong farming regime. It is possible that the expansion was in response to an increased demand for cereal generated either by an increased population, or a desire or obligation to produce an extra surplus for export. In this context the nearby Vineyard settlement at Abingdon would have been ideally placed to act as an export agent through its presumed control of river traffic.

The high level of soil nitrogen depletion evident on the site towards the end of the middle Iron Age would suggest that crop yields were probably falling rather than rising, however. Expansion of the cultivation area could, therefore, have been an increasingly desperate response to this failure rather than an attempt to raise a surplus. The decision to relocate or abandon the old settlement could be seen either as an attempt to release an area of prime quality agricultural land or ultimately as an admission that the settlement had failed.

Unlike the Ashville excavations, Wyndyke Furlong provided only limited evidence for a late Iron Age phase. It is clear that at least some of the sediment and the limestone rubble which filled the waterhole in Trench 29 (29/9) was deposited during this phase. The stone rubble suggests that the backfilling was deliberate and was probably undertaken as part of field improvement measures. Rubble of this size is unusual on Iron Age sites but its original use is unknown.

THE ROMANO-BRITISH PERIOD

Economic change and development

Although no settlement was re-established on the site, it is clear that by the late 1st century AD the land had been radically reorganised. As with the earlier settlement shift, reorganisation of the landscape during this period has previously been noted in the Upper Thames region (Lambrick 1992, 83–84). The appearance of the Roman trackway at Wyndyke and the division of land into a major field system is by no means unique in the region (Miles 1978b, 84). The change appears to reflect a move towards improved communications, greater mobility in the landscape and a growing market for livestock in new Roman towns. However, many of the changes which appear to be innovative were no more than a formalisation of existing arrangements. The suggestion that the trackway at Wyndyke may have had an Iron Age predecessor is paralleled at Farmoor where the 2nd century droveway was aligned on a route which had clearly been important as early as the middle Iron Age (Lambrick and Robinson 1979, fig. 34).

APPENDIX A: FABRIC DESCRIPTIONS

Later prehistoric *(Tables 3.1; 3.3)*

The Iron Age assemblage from Abingdon is particularly difficult to comprehensively sort into cohesive fabric groups on macroscopic examination. There is a great variety of fabrics based on the varying proportions and grades of the main constituents, namely iron, quartz sand, limestone, fossil shell and alluvial shell, and fabrics tend to merge into one another. The alluvial shell is particularly difficult to discriminate as fragments tend to be fine and sparse and the rapid method of sorting necessary will have undoubtedly overlooked some sherds.

The Iron Age fabrics have been divided into nine main ware groups:

A - calcareous (limestone only or limestone and shell-tempered)
B - sandy wares
C - sand and limestone
D - ferruginous wares (with distinct grains of iron)
E - iron and limestone-tempered
F - flint-tempered
G - grog-tempered
H - grog and limestone-tempered
I - organic.

Each group has several sub-types.
No detailed petrological work has been carried out on the wares apart from a distinctive iron oolite-tempered ware (fabric I2 below) which has been examined by Chris Doherty (Research Laboratory for Archaeology and the History of Art, Oxford University).

A. Calcareous: limestone/shell

L1: A clean, smooth, clay paste, occasionally slightly sandy with a sparse to moderate scatter of coarse fossil shell fragments up to 10 mm in size. In a finer version the fragments reach only 3–4 mm in size. Some sherds show a scatter of fine, dark coloured rounded quartz grains.

L2: A sandy textured ware, dark reddish-brown to black in colour with a sparse to moderate frequency of fine shell (probably alluvial) and occasional iron.

L3: A dark brown or black ware with sparse shell, iron and sparse visible quartz sand. The shell appears to be alluvial in many cases rather than of fossil origin. Smooth burnished finish.

L4: A reddish-brown to dark brown ware with a common frequency of fossil shell 2–3 mm in size and a prominent scatter of red-brown ferruginous compounds 2 mm in size and smaller. Fairly smooth, soapy feel.

L5: Dark brown or black ware with an oolitic-limestone temper comprising both discrete ooliths and agglomerates, rare iron and quartz sand.

L6: A black ware with a brownish interior surface. The paste contains a moderate to common frequency of greyish-white irregularly shaped limestone, rounded or oval crystalline pellets, and rare fragments of fossil shell. A scatter of rounded quartz sand can also be observed.

L7: Dark reddish-brown ware with a black core. Sparse scatter of white limestone up to 2-3 mm in size and fine quartz.

L00: Other miscellaneous limestone-tempered sherds.

B. Sandy wares

S1: Black sandy ware characterized by a moderate to common frequency of well-sorted, rounded to sub-angular, quartz sand and rare iron. A variant (S1/I) shows a scatter of fine, rounded, black iron grains difficult to pick out against the black background.

S2: A black or red-brown sandy ware with a common to moderate frequency of ill-sorted, rounded, quartz sand, the larger grains up to 1.5 mm diameter. Occasional rare iron and calcareous inclusions.

S3: A black or brown sandy ware with a scatter of fine, black or brown iron grains, 0.5 mm and less, fine mica and fine quartz sand. The iron is likely to be glauconitic indicating a likely source from the Upper Greensand series.

S4: A very fine, brown sandy ware distinguished by a finely micaceous paste. The paste includes very fine black iron grains but no other macroscopically visible inclusions.

S5: A hard, brown or grey ware characterized by a scatter of ill-sorted quartz. The larger visible grains are greyish-white, rounded and up to 2 mm in size in a dense sandy background matrix.

S6: Fine, black, sandy ware with a sparse scatter of iron, some fine mica and rare fragments of white limestone or shell.

S7: A hard, black sandy ware, sometimes with red-brown margins with a granular texture. The paste contains a common frequency of slightly ill-sorted, rounded, quartz sand.

S8: A very finely micaceous, dark brown ware. The fine sandy matrix contains a scatter of red-brown iron. Smooth burnished surfaces.

S9: Fine dark grey, sandy ware with a red haematite slipped exterior surface. Some sherds contain a small amount of limestone.

S00: Miscellaneous medium to fine dense sandy ware.

C. Sand and limestone

SL: A dark brown or black ware containing a scatter of fine, rounded quartz sand visible at x20 magnification, and sparse fine shell and limestone (less than 1 mm). In the majority of examples the shell is probably of alluvial origin. A variant is distinguished with marked iron inclusions (SL/I).

D. Ferruginous wares

I1: A dark grey or brown ware with a very iron-rich fabric. The paste contains a sparse to moderate frequency of red-orange iron rounded to sub-angular in form and 1-2 mm in size.

I2: A brownish-red ware characterized by a very distinctive temper of iron ooliths with lesser amounts of clear (monocrystalline) sub-angular quartz. There are no other ferruginous grains. Microscopic study was undertaken on this fabric by Chris Doherty (Research Laboratory for Archaeology and the History of Art, University of Oxford) who comments that the source of the iron ooliths is the Banbury outcrop of the Lower Jurassic ironstone. The rocks here consist of iron ooliths set in a matrix of limestone. On weathering and erosion the limestone is dissolved producing an oolitic gravel which may then be reworked into the alluvial clay deposits downstream of the outcrop. The abundance of ooliths in the sherds implies a clay source close to the ironstone.

E. Iron and limestone-tempered

IL1: As I2 but with a distinct presence of limestone.

IL2: As I1 but accompanied by fine fragments of limestone.

ISL: A dark brown or black ware with a composite mixture of iron, quartz sand and fossil shell/ limestone.

F. Flint-tempered

F1: A black, fine sandy ware with a common to moderate frequency of angular, white calcined flint up to 2 mm across. The paste also contains rare dark brown iron.

FI: A dark brown to black ware with a sparse frequency of white, angular, calcined flint up to 4 mm across in a iron-rich clay.

FIS: A light brown or grey ware with a common frequency of well-sorted, rounded quartz sand, a scatter of iron and rare fragments of flint (up to 5 mm) and limestone.

G. Grog-tempered

G2: Red-brown ware with a black core and interior. Smooth soapy feel, very slightly sandy. Moderate frequency of sub-angular grog, 2 mm and less in size. Handmade.

GF: A grog and flint-tempered ware.

H. Grog and limestone-tempered

GL: A red-brown ware with a black core. The paste contains a sparse to common frequency of rounded and sub-angular fragments of limestone and probably grog. These appear orange in colour on the surface and grey in fracture. Probably Bronze Age/Early Iron Age. Other variants include one with a finely micaceous paste.

I. Organic-tempered

O1: Brown surfaces with a black core and interior. Moderate to common frequency of black, quite coarse organic matter. Slightly sandy paste but no other visible inclusions.

Roman *(Table 3.4)*

Continental Imports

SAM: samian.

Regional Imports

DORBB1: Dorset black burnished ware (Williams 1977; Holbrook and Bidwell 1991).

SAVGT: Savernake ware, Wiltshire (Annable 1962).

WILRE: North Wiltshire grey sandy wares (cf Anderson 1979).

WILOX: North Wiltshire oxidised sandy wares (cf Anderson 1979).

Local wares

Grog-tempered ware

G1: Brown ware with a black core. Smooth, soapy feel. The paste contains a moderate to common frequency of sub-angular fine grog and rare red iron. Later Iron Age.

G3: Moderately hard, brownish-grey ware with a medium grey core. The paste contains a moderate frequency of subangular to angular dark grey, grog 2–3 mm in size, and rare rounded, quartz sand.

G4: Reddish-brown wheelmade grog-tempered fabric. Used for making wheelmade vessels. A similar fabric occurs at Silchester (fabric G4) (Timby forthcoming) where it dates from the early 1st century AD.

G5: A thick-walled, handmade ware, brown or grey in colour. The paste is poorly wedged with voids and contains a scatter of coarse grog/clay pellets 2-3 mm in size and finer.

G6: Wheelmade or handmade, hard, black ware with a light grey core. The paste contains a moderate frequency of dark grey subangular grog up to 3 mm in size. Used for making storage jars in the 2nd-3rd centuries.

GS1: A dark brown ware with a reddish-brown interior and a grey core. The matrix contains a scatter of rounded, greyish quartz 1 mm across and dark grey, angular grog and rare white limestone. LIA/early Roman.

GS2: A dark brownish-black ware with a brown interior. The paste contains a scatter of well-sorted quartz sand and angular orange grog up to 2-3 mm across. Wheelmade. LIA/early Roman.

GS3: A thin-walled ware with black surfaces, a reddish-orange core with a grey-brown inner core. The paste contains sparse grog, fine sand and occasional iron. Wheelmade.

Oxidised wares

OXID: Miscellaneous fine-medium sandy oxidized wares.
OXID1: A very hard, sandy ware with a grey surface and pale orange core and interior. The paste contains a dense frequency of well-sorted, quartz sand, rare large buff clay pellets and red iron.
OXIDWS: A white-slipped orange sandy ware.

Reduced wares

GREY: Miscellaneous grey sandy wares, fine-medium grades.
GREY1: A fine grey sandy ware with a red core. Few visible inclusions. (= OAU fabric R12).
GREY2: Dark grey finely micaceous ware with paler grey core. Slightly laminar/hackley fracture. The paste contains frequent fine white mica and a scatter of well-sorted, rounded, quartz grains less than 0.5 mm. Wheelmade. (= OAU fabric R50).
GREY3: A hard, medium grey ware with a lighter core. The paste contains a moderate frequency of ill-sorted quartz sand, the larger grains being very rounded with a polished appearance and reaching 2 mm in size. Rare iron. (= OAU fabric R51).
GREY4: A very fine ware with a red-brown matt surface and blue-grey core. Few visible inclusions. (= OAU fabric R52).
GREY5: A hard, dark grey ware with a lighter grey core with pinkish margins. The fabric has a fine speckled appearance from a common frequency of well-sorted fine quartz sand and rare red iron. (= OAU fabric R53).
GREY6: A black ware with a light grey core and a slightly laminar fracture. A fine sandy fabric with sparse iron. (= OAU fabric R54).
GREY7: A dark grey ware with a reddish-brown core and interior surface. A very dense sandy texture created by a common to dense frequency of well-sorted, fine, rounded quartz and a scatter of red iron. (= OAU fabric R55).
GREY8: A grey-brown ware with a black interior and a blue-grey core with brown or red-brown margins. Hard ware with a slightly laminar fracture. The paste is finely micaceous with rare rounded grains and occasional iron. (= OAU fabric R56).
GREY9: Medium-fine grey sandy ware, pale grey core, dark grey smooth exterior. Wheelmade. At x20 fabric is finely micaceous, with sparse, ill-sorted, rounded quartz grains and frequent very fine black specks (probably iron). (= OAU fabric R57).
GREY10: Dark grey ware with a red-brown core. The fabric contains a common frequency of moderately ill-sorted, sub-angular quartz sand and sparse red iron. The larger grains attain 1 mm in size, the rest is finer. (= OAU fabric R58).
GREY11: A hard, grey or reddish grey ware with a red-brown core with lighter grey inner core. A sandy texture. The only macroscopically visible inclusions are sparse rounded argillaceous grey pellets. (OAU fabric R59).

Whitewares

LOCWW: Miscellaneous white sandy wares.
LOCWW1: A fine white or pinkish white ware with a slightly chalky feel. The surfaces have a pinkish-orange bloom. At x20 a sparse scatter of fine pinkish-red grains of quartz is visible.

Oxfordshire industry wares (Young 1977)

OXFWHF: fine whiteware.
OXFWH: sandy whiteware.
OXFWHM: whiteware mortaria.
OXFRS: colour-coated ware.
OXFRE: fine grey sandy ware.
OXFOX: fine orange sandy ware.

APPENDIX B: CONCORDANCE OF CONTEXTS, FEATURES AND STRUCTURES CONTAINING ARTEFACTS AND ENVIRONMENTAL SAMPLES

Trench 29

context	feature	structure/location	figure
23/03		top soil	
29/10		well 29/9	2.1
29/12		well 29/9	2.1
29/22		well 29/9	2.1
29/23		well 29/9	2.1
29/24		well 29/9	2.1
29/25		well 29/9	2.1
29/44	cut 29/45	ditch 29/90	2.1
29/58	cut 29/57	ditch 29/88	2.1
29/75	posthole 29/74		2.1

Trench 32

context	feature	structure/location	figure
3204	ditch 3205		2.5
3216	ditch 3217	undated ditch running north-east – south-west, eastern end of site	2.3
3263	ditch 3262	between ditch 3564 and ditch 3230, north-west corner of site	2.5–2.6
3266	ditch 3261	below ditch 3564	2.5
	ditch 3303	undated ditch running north-east – south-west, eastern end of site	2.5
3329	ditch 3563		2.5
	ditch 3376	undated ditch running north-east – south-west, eastern end of site	2.5
3383	ditch 3384	undated ditch running north-east – south-west, eastern end of site	
3413	ditch 3414		2.6
	ditch 3446		2.6
3483		area of sand, north-western corner of site	2.5

Trench 33

context	feature	structure/location	figure
5002	gully 5338	post built structure 5021	2.14
5006	cut 5007	ditch 5359	2.22
5009	gully 6255	roundhouse structure 6282	2.15
5014	posthole 5015	posthole cluster 6314	2.24
5023	posthole 5024	posthole cluster 6313	2.24
5034	posthole 5035	posthole cluster 6314	2.24
5040	ditch 5043	ditch 6304	2.8
5046	pit 5048	north-east edge of gully 5338	2.14
5052	gully 5337	roundhouse structure 6282	2.15
5055	posthole 5056	posthole cluster 6314	2.14
	posthole 5088	postbuilt structure 5087	2.10
5139	gully 5141	roundhouse structure 5021	2.14
5142	gully 5340	roundhouse structure 5021	2.14
5158	pit 5157	southern edge of ditch 5832, structure 6290	2.16
	pit 5179	intersection of gullies 5342 and 6314	2.14
	posthole 5194	post-built structure 5166	2.10
5200	posthole 5201	posthole cluster 6314	2.24
5223	pit 5221		2.9
5226	posthole	post-built structure 5257	2.9–10
5227	posthole	post-built structure 5257	2.10
5231	gully 5339	roundhouse structure 5021	2.14
5238	gully 5340	roundhouse structure 5021	2.14
	posthole 5265	posthole cluster 6314	2.24

5269	pit 5270	north east edge of post-built structure 5166	2.10
5271	gully 5339	roundhouse structure 5021	2.14
5278	posthole 5279	roundhouse structure 5021	2.14
5282	pit 5511	4 m south-west of well 5664	2.19
5283	cut 5284	ditch 5359	2.22
5310	gully 5332	roundhouse structure 6282	2.15
5312	pit 5361	2 m north-east of well 5664	2.19
5321	pit 5320	near intersection of gullies 5832 and 6294, structures 6290 and 6291	2.16
5323	pit 5322	near intersection of gullies 5832 (structure 6290) and 6294 (structure 6291)	2.16
5352	cut 5353	ditch 5359	2.22
5354	cut 5355	ditch 5359	2.22
5358		ditch 5359	2.22
5360	5361	2 m north-east of well 5664	2.19
5364	pit 5372	7 m south-west of well 5664	2.19
5367	pit 5369	(on fig.)	2.16
5397	cut 5398	ditch 5359	2.22
	posthole 5434	posthole cluster 6314	2.24
5470	pit 5469	inner edge of gully 5832, opposite intersection with gully 6294	2.16
5473	pit 5478	7 m south-west of well 5664	2.19
5475	pit 5469	inner edge of gully 5832, opposite intersection with gully 6294	2.16
5476	pit 5471	near intersection of gullies 5832 (structure 6290) and 6294 (structure 6291)	2.16
5502	pit 5504	within roundhouse structure 6301	2.13
5503	pit 5504	within roundhouse structure 6301	2.13
5509	pit 5508	near intersection of gullies 5832 (structure 6290) and 6294 (structure 6291)	2.16
	pit 5522	2 m south of gully 5339, structure 5021	2.14
5524	cut 6300	ditch 6298	2.19
5533	pit 5532		2.16
5558	posthole 5561	posthole cluster 6312	2.24
5569	pit 5553		2.16
5573	pit 5553		2.16
5582	pit 5540	1 m south of well 5664	2.19
5589	cut 6299	ditch 6298	2.19
5590	cut 5595	ditch 5359	2.22
5598	cut 5599	ditch 5359	2.22
5617	cut 6299	ditch 6298	2.19
5620	cut 6300	ditch 6298	2.19
	cut 5624	ditch 6298	2.19
5627	cut 6300	ditch 6298	2.19
5637	pit 5641	7 m south-west of well 5664	2.19
5665		well 5664	2.19
5666		well 5664	2.19
5682	cut 6299	ditch 6289	2.19
	cut 5686	ditch 6298	2.19
5701	pit 5747	1 m to north of structure 6307	2.13
5702		well 5664	2.19
5704	cut 5703	ditch 5359	2.22
5706	pit 5705	within structure 6307, near southern edge of ditch 5359	2.13
5710	cut 5703	ditch 5359	2.22
5719		well 5664	2.19
5720		well 5664	2.19
5736	pit 5737	4 m south-south-east of eastern end of structure 6072	2.18
5743	pit 5740		2.18
5744		well 5664	2.19
5746	pit 5740		2.18
5757	cut 6300	ditch 6298	2.19
	cut 5779	6298	2.19
5781	cut 5703	ditch 5359	2.22
5812	gully 6219	roundhouse structure 6297	2.18
5813	gully 5815	ditched circular structure 6287	2.9

5816	gully 5832	roundhouse structure 6290	2.16
5818	pit 5817		2.11
	gully 5819	immediately to north of structure 6301	2.13
5822	cut 5703	ditch 5359	2.22
5824		well 5664	2.19
5825	pit 5845	across eastern side of gully 5846, structure 6283	2.15
	posthole 5843	windbreak 6072	2.18
5862	posthole 5863	posthole cluster 6317	2.24
5886	cut 6300	ditch 6298	2.19
5889		well 5664	2.19
5901	posthole 5900	posthole cluster 6313	
5918		well 5664	2.24
	gully 5919	within structure 6301	2.13
5922	pit 5960	2 m north-west of structure 6286	2.16
5924	pit 5923	within structure 6283	2.15
6085	cut 6084	ditch 5359	2.22
6185	posthole 6184	posthole cluster 6315	2.24
6211	cut 5709	ditch 5359	2.22
6233	cut 5709	ditch 5359	2.22
	pit 6238	8 m north-east of well 5664	2.13
6247	posthole 6206	southern edge of centre of windbreak 6072	2.18
6254	gully 6255	roundhouse structure 6282	2.15
	gully 6294	roundhouse structure 6291	2.16

Bibliography

Ainslie, R, 1992 Excavations at Thrupp near Radley, Oxon, *South Midlands Archaeol* **22**, 63-4

Allen, T G, 1990a *An Iron Age and Romano-British enclosed settlement at Watkins Farm, Northmoor, Oxon*, Thames Valley Landscapes: the Windrush Valley **1**, Oxford

Allen, T G, 1990b Abingdon Vineyard redevelopment, *South Midlands Archaeol* **20**, 73-8

Allen, T G, 1990c The Spring Road cemetery, Abingdon, Oxon, unpublished client report, Oxford Archaeological Unit

Allen, T G, 1991 An 'oppidum' at Abingdon, Oxfordshire, *South Midlands Archaeol* **21**, 97-9

Allen, T G, 1993 Abingdon Vineyard 1992: areas 2 and 3, the early defences, *South Midlands Archaeology* **23**, 64-6

Allen, T G, 1994 Abingdon, The Vineyard, area 3, *South Midlands Archaeol* **24**, 33

Allen, T G, 1995 From hamlets to oppidum, *Oxford Archaeological Unit Newsletter*, **Spring 1995**, 2-3

Allen, T G, 1996 Abingdon Vineyard, area 6 in *South Midlands Archaeol* **26**, 51-5

Allen, T G, 1997a Abingdon: west central redevelopment area, *South Midlands Archaeol* **27**, 47-54

Allen, T G, 1997b The pre-Roman pottery, in Timby *et al.* 1997, 6-7

Allen, T G, *et al.* forthcoming, *Excavations in the Vineyard, Abingdon, Oxfordshire: the Iron Age, Roman, Saxon and medieval evidence*, Thames Valley Landscapes, Oxford

Allen, T G, Miles, D, and Palmer, S, 1984 Iron Age buildings in the Upper Thames region, in Cunliffe and Miles (eds) 1984, 89-101

Allen, T G, and Robinson, M A, 1993 *The prehistoric landscape and Iron Age enclosed settlement at Mingies Ditch, Hardwick-with-Yelford, Oxon*, Thames Valley Landscapes: the Windrush Valley **2**, Oxford

Anderson, A S, 1979 *The Roman pottery industry in North Wiltshire*, Swindon Archaeological Society Report **2**, Swindon

Annable, F K, 1962 A Romano-British pottery in Savernake Forest, kilns 1-2, *Wiltshire Archaeol Mag* **58**, 142-55

Arkell, W J, 1947 *The geology of Oxford*, Oxford

Atkinson, R J C, 1952-3 Excavations in Barrow Hills Field, Radley, Berks, 1944-45, *Oxoniensia* **17-18**, 1-13

Avery, M, 1982 The Neolithic causewayed enclosure, Abingdon, in *Settlement patterns in the Oxford region: excavations at the Abingdon causewayed enclosure and other sites* (eds H J Case and A W R Whittle) CBA Res Rep **44**, 10-50, London.

Balkwill, C, 1978 The Bronze Age features, The ring ditches and their neighbourhood, and Appendix 1: a pit with Grooved Ware from Abingdon, in Parrington 1978, 25-31.

Barclay, A, in prep. The fired clay, in Allen *et al.* forthcoming

Barclay, A and Halpin, C, 1999 *Excavations at Barrow Hills, Radley, Oxfordshire* **1** *The Neolithic and Bronze Age monument complex*, Thames Valley Landscapes **11**, Oxford

Barclay, A and Lambrick, G, 1995 Berinsfield, Mount Farm, Post-excavation assessment and research design, Oxford Archaeological Unit

Barclay, A and Wait, G, forthcoming The fired clay, in *Gravelly Guy, Stanton Harcourt: the development of a prehistoric and Romano-British landscape* (G Lambrick, T Allen and F Healy), Thames Valley Landscapes, Oxford

Benson, D and Miles, D, 1974 *The Upper Thames Valley: an archaeological survey of the river gravels*, Oxford Archaeological Unit Survey **2**, Oxford

Biddle, M, Lambrick, H T and Myers, J N L, 1968 The early history of Abingdon, Berkshire, and its abbey, *Medieval Archaeology* **12**, 26-69

Booth, P M, 1997 *Asthall, Oxfordshire: excavations in a Roman 'small town'*, Thames Valley Landscapes **9**, Oxford

Booth, P M, forthcoming Report on excavations on the A 421 road alteration at Roman Alchester

Boyle, A, and Chambers, R A, in prep., The burials, in McAdam and Chambers in prep.

Bradley, P, 1999, The worked flint, in Barclay and Halpin 1999, 211-28

Bradley, P, in prep., The worked flint, in Allen *et al.* forthcoming

Bradley, P, Roe, F, and Wait, G A, forthcoming Stone, in Lambrick *et al.* forthcoming

Bradley, R, Chambers, R A, and Halpin, C E, 1984 Barrow Hills, Radley 1983-4 excavations: an interim report, unpubl. report, Oxford Archaeological Unit

Case, H, Bayne, N, Steele, S, Avery, G and Sutermeister, H, 1964-5 Excavations at City Farm, Hanborough, Oxon, *Oxoniensia* **29-30**, 1-89

Case, H J, and Whittle A W R, (eds) 1982 *Settlement patterns in the Oxford Region: excavations at the Abingdon causewayed enclosure and other sites*, CBA Res Rep **44**, London

Chambers, R A, 1985 Abingdon: Ashville Trading Estate, *Oxford Archaeological Unit Newsletter* **13(4)**, 1

Chambers, R A, 1986 Abingdon: Ashville Trading Estate, *South Midlands Archaeol* **16**, 93

Cleere, H, 1978 The slag and crucible fragments, in Parrington 1978, 88-90.

Coles, J M, 1987 *Meare Village East: the excavations of A Bullied and H St George Gray 1932-1956*, Somerset Levels Papers **13**

Cunliffe, B W, 1971 Other objects of bronze and silver, in *Excavations at Fishbourne 1961-69* **2** *The finds* (B Cunliffe), Reports of the Research Committee of the Society of Antiquaries of London, 107-26, London

Cunliffe, BW, 1984 *Danebury: an Iron Age hillfort in Hampshire* **2** *The excavations 1969-1978: the finds*, CBA Res Rep **52**, London

Cunliffe, B W, 1991 *Iron Age communities in Britain: an account of England, Scotland and Wales from the seventh century BC until the Roman conquest*, London.

Cunliffe, B W, 1996 The Danebury environs project: Suddern Farm and Fiveways excavation 1996, Internal report Danebury Trust, Oxford Institute of Archaeology

Cunliffe, B W, and Miles, D, (eds) 1984 *Aspects of the Iron Age in central southern Britain*, University of Oxford Committee for Archaeology Monograph **2**, Oxford

De Roche, C, 1978 The Iron Age pottery, in Parrington 1978, 40–74

Dickinson, T, 1976 The Anglo-Saxon burial sites Of the Upper Thames region, and their bearing on the history of Wessex, Unpubl. DPhil thesis, Univ. Oxford

Doherty, C, 1996 Comments on iron oolith tempered fabrics: OAU Iron Age sites, unpubl. research report, Oxford Archaeological Unit

Drury, P J, 1978 *Excavations at Little Waltham 1970-71*, Chelmsford Excavation Committee Report **1**, CBA Res Rep **26**, Chelmsford and London

Edwards, E, 1978 The human remains, in Parrington 1978, 90-92

Everett, R N and Eeles, R M G, 1999 Investigations at Thrupp House Farm, Radley, near Abingdon, *Oxoniensia* **64**

Fitzpatrick, A P and Morris, E L, 1994 *The Iron Age in Wessex: recent work*, Salisbury

Goodall, I H, 1990 Horseshoes, in *Object and economy in medieval Winchester* (M Biddle), 1054-67, Oxford

Grant, A, 1982 The use of tooth wear as a guide to the age of domestic ungulates, in *Ageing and sexing animal bones from archaeological sites*, (eds R Wilson, C Grigson and S Payne), BAR Brit Ser **109**, 91-108, Oxford

Grant, A, 1984a The animal husbandry, in Cunliffe 1984, 496-548

Grant, A, 1984b Animal husbandry in Wessex and the Thames Valley, in Cunliffe and Miles 1984, 102-119

Grant, A, 1989 Animals in Roman Britain, in *Research on Roman Britain 1960-89*, (ed. M Todd), Britannia Monograph Series **11**, 135-46, London

Guilbert, G, 1981 Double-ring roundhouses, probable and possible, in prehistoric Britain, *Proc Prehist Soc* **47**, 299-317.

Gwilt A and Haselgrove C C, (eds) 1997 *Reconstructing Iron Age societies: new approaches to the British Iron Age*, Oxbow Monograph **71**, Oxford

Halpin, C, 1983 Abingdon: ex-MG car factory site, *South Midlands Archaeol* **13**, 113-14

Halpin, C, 1984 Abingdon: former MG car factory, *South Midlands Archaeol* **14**, 98

Halpin, C, 1985 Abingdon: ex MG car factory, *Oxford Archaeological Unit Newsletter* **12(1)**, 1

Halpin, C, nd Summary of the results of excavation at the former MG car factory, Abingdon, unpublished report, Oxford Archaeological Unit

Hamilton, J, 1978 A comparison of the age structure at mortality of some Iron Age and Romano-British sheep and cattle populations, in Parrington 1978, 126-33

Hamilton-Dyer, S, 1995 The animal bone, in Mudd 1995, 53-4

Hey, G, Bayliss, A and Boyle, A, 1999 Iron Age inhumation burials at Yarnton, Oxfordshire, *Antiquity* **73 (281)**, 551-62

Hey, G, *et al.* in prep. a Report on excavation of the earlier prehistoric sites at Yarnton.

Hey, G, *et al.* in prep. b Report on excavation of the Iron Age and Roman sites at Yarnton.

Hill, J D, 1995 *Ritual and rubbish in the Iron Age of Wessex: a study on the formation of a specific archaeological record*, BAR Brit Ser **242**, Oxford

Hinchcliffe, J, and Thomas, R, 1980 Archaeological investigations at Appleford, *Oxoniensia* **45**, 18-73

Hingley, R, 1997 Iron, ironworking and regeneration: a study of the symbolic meaning of metalworking in Iron Age Britain, in Gwilt and Haselgrove 1997, 9-18

Hingley, R, and Miles, D, 1984 Aspects of Iron Age settlement in the Upper Thames Valley, in *Aspects of the Iron Age in central southern Britain*, (eds B Cunliffe and D Miles), University of Oxford Committee for Archaeology Monograph No. **2**, Oxford

Holbrook, N, and Bidwell, P T, 1991 *Roman finds from Exeter*, Exeter Archaeological Report **4**, Exeter

Holbrook, N, and Thomas, A, 1996 The Roman and early Anglo-Saxon settlement at Wantage, Oxfordshire: excavations at Mill Street, 1993-4, *Oxoniensia* **59**, 109-179

Holgate, R, 1988 *Neolithic settlement of the Thames basin*, BAR Brit Ser **194**, Oxford.

Holgate, R, Bradley, P, and Wallis, J, in prep. Flintwork, in *Cursus monuments in the Upper Thames valley: excavations at Drayton and Lechlade*, (A Barclay, G Lambrick, J Moore and M Robinson), Thames Valley Landscapes, Oxford

Jones, M, 1978 The plant remains, in Parrington, M 1978, 93-110.

Jones, G, Wallace, G and Skellington, W, 1980 Thrupp Farm CBA Group 9 *Newsletter* **9**, 8

Keevil, G D, 1992 An Anglo Saxon site at Audlett Drive, Abingdon, Oxon, *Oxonensia* **57**, 55-79

King, A C, 1978 A comparative survey of bone assemblages from Roman sites in Britain, *Bull Inst Archaeol Univ London* **15**, 207-32

Lambrick, G, 1979 The Iron Age pottery, in Lambrick and Robinson 1979, 35-46.

Lambrick, G, 1984 Pitfalls and possibilities in Iron Age pottery studies – experiences in the Upper Thames Valley, in *Aspects of the Iron Age in central southern Britain*, (eds B W Cunliffe, and D Miles), 162-177, Oxford

Lambrick, G, 1992 The development of late prehistoric and Roman farming on the Thames gravels, in *Developing landscapes of lowland Britain. The archaeology of the British gravels: a review*, (eds M Fulford and E Nichols), Society of Antiquaries of London Occasional Papers **14**, 77-105

Lambrick, G and Robinson, M, 1979 *Iron Age and Roman riverside settlements at Farmoor, Oxfordshire*, Oxford Archaeological Unit Report **2** and CBA Res Rep **32**, Oxford and London

Lambrick, G, Allen, T G, and Healy, F, forthcoming *Gravelly Guy, Stanton Harcourt: the development of a prehistoric and Romano-British landscape*, Thames Valley Landscapes, Oxford

Lawson, A J, 1976 Shale and jet objects from Silchester, *Archaeologia* **105**, 241-74

MacGregor, A, 1985 *Bone, antler, ivory and horn*, London

Manning, W H, 1985 *Catalogue of the Romano-British iron tools, fittings and weapons in the British Museum*, London

McAdam E, and Chambers, R A, in prep., *Excavations at Barrow Hills, Radley, Oxfordshire* **2** *The Roman and Saxon evidence*

Miles, D, 1978a The Roman pottery, in Parrington 1978, 74-8

Miles, D, 1978b The Upper Thames Valley, in *Early land allotment*, (eds H C Bowen and P J Fowler), BAR Brit Ser **48**, Oxford

Miles, D, 1986 *Archaeology at Barton Court Farm, Abingdon, Oxon*, Oxford Archaeological Unit Report **3**, CBA Res Rep **50**, Oxford and London

Morris, E 1985 Prehistoric salt distributions: two case studies from western Britain, *Bulletin of the Board of Celtic Studies* **32**, 336-379

Morris, E forthcoming Briquetage, in *Gravelly Guy, Stanton Harcourt: the development of a prehistoric and Romano-British landscape* (G Lambrick, T Allen and F Healy), Thames Valley Landscapes, Oxford

Mudd, A, 1993 Excavations at Whitehouse Road, Oxford, 1992, *Oxoniensia* **58**, 33-85

Mudd, A, 1995 The excavation of a late Bronze Age/early Iron Age site at Eight Acre Field, Radley, *Oxoniensia* **60**, 21-65

Oswald, A, 1997 A doorway on the past: practical and mystic concerns in the orientation of roundhouse doorways, in *Reconstructing Iron Age societies*, (eds A Gwilt and C C Haselgrove), Oxbow Monograph **71**, 87-95, Oxford

Parkinson, A, Barclay, A and McKeague, P, 1996 The excavation of two Bronze Age barrows, Oxford, *Oxoniensia* **59**, 41-64

Parrington, M, 1978, *The excavation of an Iron Age settlement, Bronze Age ring ditches and Roman features at Ashville Trading Estate, Abingdon, Oxfordshire, 1974-76*, Oxford Archaeological Unit Report **1**, CBA Res Rep **28**, Oxford and London

Pitts, M W, and Jacobi, R M, 1979 Some aspects of change in flaked stone industries of the Mesolithic and Neolithic of southern Britain, *Journal of Archaeological Science* **6**, 166-170

Pocock, T I, 1926 *The geology of the country around Oxford*, Memoirs of the Geological Survey, England, explanation of Special Oxford Sheet, London

Poole, C, 1984, Clay weights, in *Danebury: an Iron Age hillfort in Hampshire*, **2** *The excavations 1969-1978: the finds.* CBA Res Rep **52**, 400-406, London

Roberts, M, 1993 *Plot A, Abingdon Business Park (former MG Works)*, unpubl. evaluation report, Oxford Archaeological Unit

Roberts, M, 1994 *Wyndyke Furlong, Abingdon Business Park, Abingdon, Oxfordshire*, unpubl. evaluation report, Oxford Archaeological Unit

Roberts, M, 1995 'Back to our roots: Ashville and Wyndyke' in *Oxford Archaeological Unit Newsletter* **Spring 1995**

Roe, F, 1995 The worked stone, in Walker 1995, 84

Roe, F, 1996 Stone objects, in Holbrook and Thomas, 1996, 152-154

Roe, F, 1997 Worked stone (except flint), in Booth 1997, 100-101

Roe, F, 1999, Worked stone, in Barclay and Halpin 1999, 82

Roe, F, forthcoming a, The worked stone, in Lambrick, Allen and Healy forthcoming

Roe, F, forthcoming b, The worked stone, in Allen *et al.* forthcoming

Roe, F, forthcoming c, The worked stone, in Booth forthcoming

Roe, F, in prep. a, Report on worked stone, in Hey *et al.* in prep a.

Roe, F, in prep. b, Report on worked stone, in Hey *et al.* in prep. b.

Sellwood, L, 1984 Objects of bone and antler, in *Danebury: an Iron Age hillfort in Hampshire* **2** *The excavations 1969-1978: the finds* (B Cunliffe), CBA Res Rep **52**, 371-95, London

Shand, P, 1985 Corporation Farm, Abingdon: excavations of late Neolithic monuments and middle Bronze Age rectilinear enclosures 1970-71, unpubl. undergraduate dissertation, Univ. Reading

Skellington, W A, 1978 The worked flints, in Parrington 1978, 90-91

Timby, J R, 1995 The pottery, in Walker 1995, 78-82

Timby, J R, forthcoming The pottery, in *Late Iron Age and Roman Silchester: excavations on the site of the forum-basilica, 1977-86* (M Fulford and J Timby), Britannia Monograph **15**, London

Timby, J R, Booth, P, and Allen, T G, 1997 A new early Roman fineware industry in the Upper Thames Valley, unpubl. report, Oxford Archaeological Unit

Trust for Wessex Archaeology, 1996 Clarendon to Cockey Down Water Main, Salisbury, Wiltshire, Internal report prepared for Wessex Water, Trust for Wessex Archaeology

Walker, G T, 1995 A middle Iron Age settlement at Deer Park farm, Witney: excavations in 1992, *Oxoniensia* **60**, 67-92

Whittle, A W R, 1986 Struck flint, in Miles 1986, M3B5-3B10

Williams, D F, 1977 The Romano-British black-burnished industry: an essay in characterization by heavy mineral analysis, in *Pottery and early commerce: characterization and trade in Roman and later ceramics* (ed. D P S Peacock), 163-220, London

Wilson, D, 1993 Iron Age pottery, in Allen and Robinson 1993, 70-5

Wilson, R, 1978 Sampling bone densities at Mingies Ditch, Oxfordshire, in *Sampling in contemporary British Archaeology*, (eds J F Cherry, C Gamble and S Shennan) BAR Brit Ser **50**, 355-62, Oxford

Wilson, R, 1985 Degraded bones, feature type and spatial patterning on an Iron Age occupation site in Oxfordshire, England, in *Palaeobiological investigations: research design, methods, and data analysis*, (eds N J R Fieller, D D Gilbertson and N G Ralph), BAR Int Ser **266**, 81-96, Oxford

Wilson, R, 1992 Considerations for the identification of ritual deposits of animal bones in Iron Age pits, in *International Journal of Osteoarchaeology* **2**, 341-349

Wilson, R, 1993 Reports on the bone and oyster shell, in Allen and Robinson, 1993, 123-134

Wilson, R, 1996 *Spatial patterning among animal bones in settlement archaeology*, BAR Brit Ser **251**, Oxford

Wilson, R, 1997 Aspects of animal life and death in an Iron Age settlement at Tuckwell's Pit near Radley, Oxon, *Oxoniensia* **62**, 313-319

Wilson, R, and Allison, E, 1990 The animal and fish bones, in Allen 1990a, 57-61

Wilson, R and Bramwell, D, 1979 The vertebrates, in Lambrick and Robinson 1979, 128-133

Wilson, R, Hamilton, J, Bramwell, D and Armitage, P, 1978 The animal bones, in Parrington 1978, 110-139

Young, C J, 1977 *Oxfordshire Roman pottery*, BAR Brit Ser **43**, Oxford